Richard Bean

ENGLAND PEOPLE VERY NICE

OBERON BOOKS
LONDON

First published in 2009 by Oberon Books Ltd
521 Caledonian Road, London N7 9RH
Tel: 020 7607 3637 / Fax: 020 7607 3629
e-mail: info@oberonbooks.com
www.oberonbooks.com

Reprinted 2009, 2011

A catalogue record for this book is available from the British
Library.

ISBN: 978-1-84002-900-0

Cover design by Michael Mayhew

Printed in Great Britain by CPI Antony Rowe Ltd, Chippenham.

Freedom is the freedom to say that two plus two make four.
George Orwell (*1984*)

Characters

A large, ethnically mixed company of actors is needed.
Some characters are recurring.

RECURRING CHARACTERS

NORFOLK DANNY / CARLO / AARON / MUSHI, 20s
The boy lover

CAMILLE / MARY / RUTH / DEBORAH, 20s
The girl lover

IDA, Pub barmaid

LAURIE, Pub landlord

RENNIE, Pub regular, originally from Barbados

CORE CAST FOR PROLOGUE / EPILOGUE –
ALTHOUGH ALL PLAYERS ARE PRESENT

YAYAH, Male Nigerian

PHILIPPA, Female English

ELMAR, Male Azerbaydzhan

TAHER, Male Palestinian

SANYA, Female Kosovan

IQBAL, Male Yemen

OFFICER KELLY, Male Ulster

OFFICER PARKER, Male English

TATYANA, Female Serbian

GINNY, Female English, stage manager

SET / STAGING

The play requires a large stage with the facility to fly in flats, or use still, or video projections, to establish locations as required. This process should be playful and non-naturalistic. The only constant location is the pub, which can be naturalistic.

England People Very Nice was first performed at the Olivier Theatre, National Theatre, on 4 February 2009, with the following cast:

Philip Arditti
Jamie Beamish
Paul Chequer
Olivia Colman
Rudi Dharmalingam
Sacha Dhawan
Hasina Haque
Tony Jayawardena
Trevor Laird
Elliot Levey
Siobhán McSweeney
Neet Mohan
Aaron Neil
Sophia Nomvete
Daniel Poyser
Claire Prempeh
Fred Ridgeway
Avin Shah
Sophie Stanton
Michelle Terry
David Verrey
Harvey Virdi

Director Nicholas Hytner
Designer Mark Thompson
Director of Animation Pete Bishop
Lighting Designer Neil Austin
Music Grant Olding
Choreographer Scarlett Mackmin
Sound Designer John Leonard

Prologue

A bare stage.

GINNY: (*Off.*) Full company to the stage please!

The company of actors breeze on. Other asylum seekers enter accompanied by Immigration Centre Officers. They are in costume, depicting the early history of Britain – Angles, Vikings, Saxons, Celts, etc.

PHILIPPA: NOTES! It's almost…quite good.

A mobile phone is heard. It's YAYAH's. He's dressed as a Roman centurion with short sword, skirt, etc. He gives the short sword to a fellow asylum seeker and answers his phone.

YAYAH: (*On phone.*) Of course it's me woman!… Listen! I am not in Lagos so you will have to beat the girl yourself! Goodbye, I am in a meeting!

PHILIPPA: Tatyana, no smoking please! Pocklington Immigration Centre is a place of work!

TATYANA: Where can I smoke?

PHILIPPA: Nowhere in England. Today we're going to do a dress rehearsal working with Elmar's animation, I've seen it, it's absolutely amazing!

ELMAR: Every year in Azerbaydzhan I win the Silver Dragon for animated short.

TAHER: Who wins gold?

ELMAR: In Azerbaydzhan silver is first prize, if you win gold, you've come second.

PHILIPPA: Unfortunately, for us, Doctor Kuti has been given leave to remain. So Taher will now give his St John, the sarcastic army-trained Hampstead liberal who gets mugged.

TAHER: If Doctor Kuti has had his envelope, all the envelopes must be here?

PHILIPPA: Mister Kelly!?

OFFICER KELLY: The strike is over, yeah, but I don't know anything about envelopes.

TAHER: Our cases were heard – [in October]

YAYAH: – Sit down man! You're pissing me off! We have a show to do!

ELMAR: In Azerbaydzhan we have a saying, 'eating fish will not improve your swimming'.

PHILIPPA: Today we have music, the Pocklington Immigration Centre Officers officers' band.

A roll on the drums. And messy contributions from the band. Applause from the players.

What else?

GINNY: (*Distort / Off.*) Nazeerah!

PHILIPPA: Thanks Ginny. Miss Gupta has 'Home Office' interviews so I will take over the demanding roles of Mrs O'Neill and Camilla.

TATYANA: Camilla, the idiot!?

PHILIPPA: Yes. OK notes! Sanya?! Problem. I can hear the swearing. Ida is white working class Bethnal Green. To her 'facking', is not swearing – it's punctuation.

SANYA: FUCKING frogs!

PHILIPPA: No! Pong 'Frogs'. Pong – theatrical term, emphasise Frogs.

SANYA: Fucking FROGS! Fucking MICKS! Fucking YIDS! Fucking PAKIS!

PHILIPPA: Perfect!

TAHER: Swearing is the truth, of course, when I worked in Israeli theatre I notice they swear all the time, but do Israelis care a shit about the truth –

PHILIPPA: – Taher! If you mention Israel today, you're back in your cell. Can I do that, Mister Kelly?

OFFICER KELLY: Do what you like love.

TAHER: Gitmo!

PHILIPPA: If you'd like to go to Guantanamo Bay it can be arranged. Yayah?! Your line 'turn your mobile phones off please', be more threatening, as if something really really terrible might happen to them.

YAYAH: More threatening. Easy peasey!

PHILIPPA: Iqbal. You've shaved your beard off. Your beard was the reason we cast you as the mad imam.

GINNY: (*Distort/Off.*) Props don't have any more false beards.

IQBAL: I kept the hair, and last night I sat up and made a beard wig.

He puts a false beard on.

YAYAH: Ey! It looks just like your old beard.

IQBAL: Of course it does, it is my old beard.

ELMAR: In Azerbaydzhan we have a saying, 'don't expect miracles from a beard, it's only facial hair'.

TAHER: England is a free country, you're allowed to have a beard.

TATYANA: Why don't you have a beard? You're Palestinian.

TAHER: I'm a Christian! The reason I am seeking asylum in this country is because Hamas want to kill me for not having a beard.

YAYAH: I know why Hamas want to kill you, it's because you talk too much!

TATYANA: Go to Scotland, you can wear a dress too!

PHILIPPA: Stop! You've spent six months devising this play. Six months learning how England became a liberal, tolerant, democratic society. It would be a shame to cancel the show, but I can, because the work was in the work.

IQBAL: You had a note for me Philippa.

PHILIPPA: Yes, er… (*Reading.*) when you first come on can you try and not look like a…oh yes I remember…it doesn't matter now.

IQBAL: Not look like a what?

PHILIPPA: You've shaved the beard off now so it doesn't matter.

TATYANA: Not look like a mad dog!

PHILIPPA: Tatyana! Please.

TAHER: My idea for the Saudi Imam when I wrote it –

YAYAH: – you did not write that bit, it is all devised, by us. Collectively.

TAHER: The group turned my imam into a stereotype – mad, blind, hooks for hands. The imam will be better without the beard and the beard wig.

TATYANA: It is not a stereotype, they've all got beards!

PHILIPPA: Quiet! Please!

SANYA: Philippa, I don't think my character would say 'vis à vis'? She's a barmaid.

PHILIPPA: We took a democratic vote, to close all discussion on the script.

TAHER: She is third generation French. 'Vis à vis' is French.

PHILIPPA: Taher, just try not to help OK? The Irish act. Where are the Houlihans?

HOULIHANS: Aye / Hallooo there! / What now then!? So…

PHILIPPA: Really, really, terrific accent work!

HOULIHAN 1: We've worked on our *Oirish* with Officer Kelly there, aye we have so…

OFFICER KELLY: I'm from the north meself Miss, but me family is from Knocknagree, I mean I know it's not Galway, but it's better than a kick in the clems. And Geoff, Officer Parker, he's been working on their cockney.

OFFICER PARKER: Awight! That kind of thing.

COCKNEYS: Awight! / Wotcha! / Fack off! *etc.*

PHILIPPA: What can I say, fantastic! Now Houlihans, I need to believe that it's normal for your family to have a pig in the house. What I'm getting at the moment is – *'hey hey! we're the Houlihans! Look! We're all mad, and we got a fecking pig in the house!'*

HOULIHANS: Aye! / Right you are there! / No problem so!

TAHER: I research Irish Famine on Wikipedia. Irish Famine 1840! The Gordon riots 1780. In this play the two things happen in the same afternoon. Sixty years wrong!

PHILIPPA: Shakespeare had a clock in *Julius Caesar*. One thousand years wrong! Now, we might have an audience today, my husband, if you hear laughing, or crying, he cries easily, it's him.

TATYANA: Maybe he will snore all the way through.

PHILIPPA: There is no chance of that.

ELMAR: What's his name?

PHILIPPA: St John.

TAHER: Does he understand theatre?

PHILIPPA: No, he works for Vodafone. OK! Set for a run!

GINNY: (*Distort/Off.*) The wagon joke!

PHILIPPA: Yes, the wagon joke is back in.

TAHER: We are putting a joke back in which is not funny?

PHILIPPA: Taher, if we let you stay in this country, and after thirty years working as a driving instructor in Kettering you develop a drink problem – a) you'll understand the joke, and b) you'll find it funny!

GINNY: (*Distort/Off.*) Can we run the wagon joke lines. 'Oi mate'.

ADRIANA: Oi mate! Do you want a drink?

YAYAH: No, ta. I can't. I'm on the wagon.

TAHER: It is not funny!

PHILIPPA: Check your props! Alright in the box!?

They exit the stage and prepare their props etc.

Song: 'A True Born Londoner'
(After Defoe's 'The True Born Englishman')

> This stage depicts an age bygone
> The Thames before Londinium
> A leaky shack to call our home
> No cars no bars no mobile phone

YAYAH: Turn your mobiles off please. (*Beat.*) Or else.

> There is no Christ, nor even God
(*Chalk giants.*) But pagan giants Gog and Magog
(*Enter iron age man.*) This beast exemplar is the height
(*And wife.*) And this, his cousin, is his wife

> With a ro do a derry diddle diddle do
> A ro do derry diddle di

(Enter Roman.)	First came the Roman with his rule
(Stabs man.)	And steeled the cockney with his tool
(Rapes woman.)	This seminal act improved the tribe
(Literate man/wife.)	And issued forth a learned scribe
(Men killed...)	The Saxons came, and came again
(Same woman raped.)	Were followed by the lusty Dane
(Men killed.)	They fought and fought eternal wars
(Woman raped again.)	The ladies loved the conquerors

With a ro do a derry diddle diddle do
A ro do derry diddle di
With a ro do a derry diddle diddle do
A ro do derry diddle di

(And so on...)   The western Angles beat the lot
With the exception of the Scot
The warlike Celt under foot was
   squelched
And fleeing West became the Welsh
With a ro do a derry diddle diddle do
A ro do derry diddle di
With a ro do a derry diddle diddle do
A ro do derry diddle di

Enter NORFOLK DANNY in his 17th century incarnation as a Journeyman weaver in Spitalfields.

This God resulting is our play
Four hundred years we'll roll away
A weaver, not poor, but not well heeled
A Norfolk man in Spitalfields

Act One

17th century Spitalfields. Fields and trees for the outskirts. The Tower of London dominates the skyline. Street life. The STREET VENDORS sing their cries. The TOWN CRIER ringing a bell.

SEA COALS: Sea coals! Come on mother, sort it out!

BEGGAR: Any spare farthings sir?

CRIER: Get a craft you lazy bastard! Oyez! Oyez! Oyez!

ALL: (*Joining in after the second.*) Oyez! Oyez!

CRIER: Following the Revocation of the Edict of Nantes by Louis the Fourteenth of France –

SEA COALS: – France!?

SAUSAGES: What's this got to do with us?

CRIER: – the Protestant Reformed Religion has been prohibited in that land. London is forewarned of a swarming.

CRIER starts to walk off.

SEA COALS: Swarming of what?!

CRIER: Frogs!

During the song the French arrive. Houses are built and they move in.

Frogs song (After traditional anti-French song of the time)

A plague of Frogs do come and live at ease
And fatter look than wretched refugees
Our English weavers all do curse their fates
The French will work for lower rates
Kindly protected from the stroke
Of Louis' Roman Cath'lic hawk

Them we so well will entertain
They will not choose go home again
And over time now the French rise high
As we sing our carping cry
And as they have all Merchant Masters made
And like the free born English, trade

In the pub.

IDA: Fucking frogs! My grandfather didn't die in the English Civil War so's half of France could come over here and live off the soup!

LAURIE: Your grandfather didn't die in the English Civil War. He was in here yesterday.

IDA: That's what I said. I said 'my grandfather *didn't die* in the English Civil War so's half of France could come here and live off the soup.

RENNIE: I've got Frogs upstairs from me boy! All day long – farting, farting, farting!

LAURIE: This is a small island knowhatimean?!

RENNIE: They eat nothing but red meat and cabbage!

LAURIE: (*Re: pamphlet.*) That writer, Daniel Defoe, says here we shouldn't mind living cheek by jowl with fifty thousand foreigners.

IDA: Alright for him, he'll be glad of the company, he's spent the last twenty-eight years on a fucking desert island!

RENNIE: All them dissident writers! They don't have to live here boy!

IDA: By the time the bells go of a night, they're all back in Stoke Newington with all their lovely whatsanames –

LAURIE: – trees.

IDA: Fucking trees!

Enter DANNY.

LAURIE: Alright Norfolk?!

DANNY: Pint of Mad Dog please. What's new?

LAURIE: There is a great noise upon the land, the farting of a million Froglanders.

RENNIE: There'll be rivers of blood boy! War, across Europe!

DANNY: Religion you see.

LAURIE: I'll have none of your Reincarnation Society 'God is Dead' talk until you've coughed up the money for the room rental from last Tuesday.

DANNY gives LAURIE half a shilling. He takes it.

DANNY: God is Dead.

IDA and RENNIE laugh.

IDA: You'll never find yerself a nice girl, wiv all this Godlessness. You might as well go round shouting 'Plague!' And ringing a fucking whatsaname –

LAURIE: – bell.

RENNIE: All that red meat boy! Makes French girls hot. I mean hot, hot, hot!

IDA: What you need Danny, is a nice English girl who don't like sex. You'll be alright though son, you got your own loom now, ain'tcher!?

RENNIE: Life begins when you get your own loom boy!

LAURIE: What you on Norfolk? Silk?

DANNY: Yeah, narrow silk, with fancy trimming.

RENNIE: French men, they're worse! They eat that red meat raw!

LAURIE: Our girls ain't gonna be safe from Gallic overexcitement even in church.

SIDNEY DE GASCOIGNE meets with the BISHOP. He has his son with him. They've been eating.

BISHOP: Exactly how big will this big French church be?

DE GASCOIGNE: I would expect a congregation of two thousand.

DENHAM: Your grace, they have petitioned plans for a school.

DE GASCOIGNE: We want to teach our children French, so that they can recite the catechism – in French.

BISHOP: What makes you so sure that God speaks French? A child born in London is not French. He is irretrievably an Englishman, and 'gawd 'elp us all', a cockney. At least the moral health of Londoners will be protected if you have your own church. More beef?

DE GASCOIGNE: Not for me thank you. I can't speak for my son. Yves?

GASKIN: Non, merci.

BISHOP: Bit overcooked was it?

GASKIN: C'est bon.

BISHOP: You may cling to your Frenchness now, but I'll wager you die an Englishman.

DE GASCOIGNE: I don't gamble.

BISHOP: What's crossing the English channel in a barrel if not gambling?

DE GASCOIGNE: These barrel stories, are exaggerated. I paid passage from Dieppe.

DENHAM: How prosaic.

BISHOP: You have fled Catholic France and as Protestants we welcome you as brothers, but England has many surreptitious Catholics. Not all Catholics are violent Papists, BUT all violent Papists are Catholics. Our King is Catholic; however, he has a Protestant son-in-law, William of Orange –

DE GASCOIGNE: – Is this a prophesy or a plot?

BISHOP: If he were to become King, William will lead us in war against France. Will you cheer for England or cheer for France?

DE GASCOIGNE: That would be a test.

A huge church appears.

BLACKAMOOR: Turkish coffee boss?! Knock your block off coffee!

DANNY stands looking at the church. An Englishman walks past the church protecting his daughter from a group of young French men. CAMILLE, a French girl, makes eye contact with DANNY. The Lovers' musical theme plays.

CAMILLE: Hello!

DANNY: Bonjour! Comment ça va?

CAMILLE: You speak French sir?

DANNY: Un peu. Not really.

CAMILLE: Camille. Camille de Chaunay. My brother, André.

DANNY: Danny. They call me Norfolk Danny because I'm Norfolk bred and born.

CAMILLE: Au revoir, Norfolk Danny.

CAMILLE goes in to the church. DANNY stands at the back.

DE GASCOIGNE: (*Heavy French accent.*) Monsieurs dames, mes amis, bonjour, welcome, for the first time, to this house of God which we have so imaginatively called

the French Church. I am the prologue to the sermon,
I will be quick. Like you, I am here in Brick Lane, in
England this foul smelling swamp, only because I want
to worship my God free from the constraints of Papal
instruction, and the threat of death. Like lovers in exile,
we must maintain French culture. The English are drunks,
incapable of intellectual discourse, they make a god of
common sense, they hate their children, and would always
rather be 'unting. We French, are superior in all things,
watchmaking, textiles, armoury, and, of course, love.

There is uncontrolled sighing in the congregation.

Londoners fear our style, our sophistication, our
romancing. They will not allow us through the gates
into the city. So outside the walls, right here, let's build
French homes, in streets with French names, and through
extraordinary and relentless love making, let us populate
these streets with French children and create a new Nîmes,
a new Perpignan, a new Paris!

*DANNY leaves. A gang of apprentices armed with knives and scissors
arrive. CAMILLE watches.*

HUGO: One on one, the Frogs, they're fucking nothing!

BENNY: Norfolk Danny! Have you paid your shilling?

DANNY: I've paid my two shilling Guild sub yeah.

DICK: Extra shilling now innit. Protection. Against the French.

DANNY: So this is a cutters' mob?

BENNY: They've started up with their own looms, paying fuck
all wages.

DANNY: We can't have that can we…

*DANNY pays his shilling. A Frenchman walks by holding a roll of
cloth.*

FRENCH MAN: Bonjour!

HUGO: Stand and fight you fucking cabbage eating farting Frog Papist!

DANNY: Papist? They're not Catholics!

HUGO: Frog lover now eh, Norfolk?

DANNY: They're Huguenots, Protestants, they follow John Calvin.

BENNY: Not Godless then, like you.

DANNY: Let's smash their looms, that's reasonable. But I'm not kicking a Protestant in the head for being Papist.

CAMILLE has seen this. She follows DANNY back to his cottage. Her brother ANDRÉ is in tow.

CAMILLE: You are a weaver?

DANNY: Yeah, I'm a Journeyman, got me own loom.

HUGO: Hang on to your pants Danny! Them French girls, knowhatimean!?

DANNY: You speak really good English.

CAMILLE: It was this facility that saved me. My mother is dead, and my father condemned to the galleys for a hundred years.

DANNY: Yeah? That's a lot of rowing.

HUGO goes off.

CAMILLE: Sir, do not mock me!

DANNY: I'm sorry, he was watching. He's Guild you see.

CAMILLE: What cloth do you weave?

DANNY: Narrow silk with fancy trimming.

CAMILLE: André, my brother, is apprenticed to the finest Master of Nîmes, making this cloth, Serge de Nîmes.

She gives DANNY a sample of denim.

CAMILLE: Two white vertical threads –

DANNY: – the warps. The warp goes to the top, the weft goes right to left.

DANNY uses his fingers to illustrate the warps. CAMILLE creates a weft with her own finger.

CAMILLE: A lone, weft, dyed blue completes the weave. De Nîmes.

DANNY: Denîmes? Coarse. Alright for work clothes. Can't see it ever catching on.

DANNY gives the denim back. ANDRÉ passes to CAMILLE another sample. She shows DANNY.

Silk?

CAMILLE: No! Bombasin. The warp is silk but the weft is wool.

DANNY: That's amazing.

CAMILLE: My brother can make this for you. And I could help your wife sir.

DANNY: Come to my house.

They go in.

The loom's atop, in the attic.

CAMILLE: Monte! Va vérifier le métier!

ANDRÉ climbs the stairs.

DANNY: I don't have a wife.

CAMILLE: Oh! I excel at all those labours that a woman of limited means might reasonably be expected to perform.

DANNY: You talk like a lady. I'm only a Journeyman.

CAMILLE: But you are not like the mob, I can tell, you have had an education –

DANNY: I was to be a priest. It's a narrow schooling and don't make me a gentleman.

CAMILLE: Your station does not interest me. I'm alive. My brother and I are the human jetsam of this conflict between my poor dead father, and the Pope.

DANNY: You said your father was on the galleys.

CAMILLE: He could never conform to the regime, and will surely now…be dead.

DANNY: And your mother?

CAMILLE: Beheaded.

DANNY: By religious men.

CAMILLE: Are you a Protestant sir?

DANNY: Neither Catholic nor Protestant. In the seminary I sought harder than any man, and with great confidence. And found nothing.

CAMILLE: But without God –

DANNY: – I'm lawless, wretched, and free. Have you ever taken all the fear and threats out of your heart, and using reason alone, have you questioned the existence of God?

CAMILLE: That would make me a heretic.

DANNY: That's me. That's what you're getting into. How did you escape France?

CAMILLE: In Marseille we stowed away on a ship bound for London but the jack o' tars found me, and ooh –

She collapses, and is caught by DANNY, enter ANDRÉ.

ANDRÉ: Le métier, c'est de la merde.

DANNY: What's he say?

CAMILLE: He says the loom is perfect.

ANDRÉ: Je vais me tirer pour tu fasses ton truc?

CAMILLE: Ne mets pas les pieds dans le pub. Allez!

ANDRÉ takes a penny from CAMILLE and then he leaves.

DANNY: I can offer you a roof and a meal. I can't pay André wages, the Guild –

CAMILLE: – Bon! I will sleep here. Where will you sleep?

DANNY: Are you promised?

CAMILLE: I can never return. I saw my mother's corpse dragged behind a little pony, the rope tight around her neck, the blood, the dust.

DANNY: When the sailors found you…on the ship?

CAMILLE: I traded my honour for my life.

DANNY: I'm sorry.

DANNY picks up a framed document on the wall.

This is the Guild ordinance. Rules for everything.

Reading 'No single man, shall take to his house a lecher'.

CAMILLE: Is that what I am to you? A French whore?

DANNY: You're a woman, and you're not my wife.

CAMILLE: No-one can legislate for love!

DANNY: Love?!

CAMILLE: Yes, love! I will cook, and sew for you, our proximity will nurture feelings of lust, and we will fall in love. Do you not understand it is inevitable? Tomorrow you will swim the seven seas for one more kiss.

DANNY: I can't swim.

CAMILLE: Agh! It's true what they say about the English. You care nothing for love! We French are wasting our time here!

Bells sound.

DANNY: Curfew.

CAMILLE: Bed time?

DANNY: Yeah. Now, tell me the truth.

CAMILLE: I beg your pardon.

DANNY: One minute you say your mother was beheaded, the next minute she's getting dragged through the streets behind a pony with the rope round her neck, 'the blood', 'the dust'.

CAMILLE: Our fathers do get condemned to the galleys, and our mothers are beheaded, their bodies dragged through the streets!

DANNY: But not yours!

CAMILLE: I first exaggerated my father's plight, the galleys, with the sea captain. He had heard of that punishment for Protestants and was –

DANNY: – easily deceived.

CAMILLE: My inventions earned us a cabin.

DANNY: A cabin! So I'm just the last in a long line of mugs.

CAMILLE: All that matters is that I still breathe.

DANNY: Like a hawk sees a vole, deep in the roots of the corn, you saw my need for a woman.

Outside the cutters' MOB return, bloody, and drunk.

MOB: Rule, Britannia! Britannia rules the waves
Britain never never never will be slaves
Rule, Britannia! Britannia rule the waves
Britain never never never will be slaves!

They spot ANDRÉ hiding from them.

BEN: (*To ANDRÉ.*) Oi! Mate! You're not singing!?

DICK picks some threads off his coat.

ANDRÉ: Je ne parle pas Anglais.

HUGO: Look! He got threads on his coat!

BENNY: Whose loom are you working? Me, name, Benny. Your master? Name?

ANDRÉ: Danné.

HUGO: Norfolk Danny!?

BENNY: Won't be Norfolk. What type of cloth? Cloth!? (*Tugs his clothes.*)

ANDRÉ: Soie.

HUGO: Silk.

BENNY: What kind of soie? (*Mimes.*) Broad?

ANDRÉ: (*Mimes narrow.*) Non. Étroit.

BENNY: Narrow.

ANDRÉ: – avec… (*Mimes fancy trimming.*)

BENNY: Narrow silk with fancy trimming!

HUGO: Norfolk Danny! Let's kill the bastard!

In DANNY's.

CAMILLE: You have a need for a woman, I have a need for a man.

DANNY moves to kiss her but before he can BENNY and HUGO crash in.

DANNY: Did you want to talk to me Benny?

BENNY: Guild rules Norfolk, you can't have a whore indoors.

DANNY: I'm gonna make her my wife.

BENNY: And how you gonna provide for her after we've smashed your loom up?

HUGO: Let's have a feel darling!

HUGO grabs CAMILLE, DANNY rushes HUGO with his own shears, and stabs him.

HUGO: He done me!

BENNY: Jesus! You'll swing Norfolk, you'll swing mate.

HUGO: I want me muvver! Benny, mate, go get me muvver! Quick, please.

HUGO dies. DANNY picks up the bloody shears, and threatens the others.

DANNY: Who's next? Benny?! I will. They can only hang me once.

BENNY leaves.

Camille! Leave, go to Canterbury. I'll find you.

CAMILLE: Danny? I need to know. Do you love me?

DANNY: Stop talking about bloody love! Go! Run!

CAMILLE: I'll find you. If it takes a four hundred years, I'll find you.

CAMILLE runs off.

CRIER: Oyez! Oyez! Oyez! On this the twenty-third day of February in the year of our lord sixteen eighty-nine – James Stuart –

ALL: Papist / traitor! / dog! / Boo!

CRIER: – having fled his kingdom to take refuge in Catholic France –

ALL: Boo!

CRIER: – His daughter Mary and her husband, William of Orange, lead their subjects in military opposition to Catholic France.

SEA COALS: What's that in English?!

CRIER: We're at war with France!

ALL: War! / War with France!

The French congregation gather.

DE GASCOIGNE: Watcha! Turned out nice again! Cheer up
love, it might never happen! Worse things happen at
sea! Yes, I am speaking English! If you have difficulty
understanding me I might ask you why. Some of you
still have the fleurs de lis tattooed on your hearts. Your
children, born here, cockaneeys, still speak French – why?
France rejected you like a girl rejects a lover. A new
page in history is writ today. England is at war with
your sweetheart. I implore you not to give the English
permission to question your loyalty! I am no longer Sidney
de Gascoigne. From this day forth, I am brutal, short,
pragmatic, Bert. Yes, Bert Gaskin, and my son Al-bert
Gaskin. And I implore you all to similarly Anglicise your
reputations.

Murmurs of disapproval.

I do this because she, France, broke my heart, but England,
she offered me her bosoms!

MOB: A hanging! A hanging!

*A cart with scaffold is pulled on. DANNY is running along behind
the wagon, his hands are tied together and he is roped to the wagon.
Travelling on the cart with them is the HANGMAN and a JUDGE /
OFFICIAL. Some SOLDIERS to keep the peace.*

SAUSAGES: Danny! Do you wanna drink!?

DANNY: Yeah!

They give DANNY a drink.

MOB / ALL: A drink! / Ale.

SEA COALS: (*To HANGMAN.*) Oi! Mate, do you want a drink?

HANGMAN: No, ta. I can't. I'm on the wagon.

DANNY is hauled up on to the wagon.

BEGGAR: Speech! Speech!

BENNY: You'll rot in hell Norfolk Danny!

DANNY: There is no hell! Nor heaven! This is the only
paradise any of you will ever know.

IDA: What? Bethnal Green?

DANNY: Yes!

IDA: Where's your girl Danny?

DANNY: I don't know. I did not even kiss her, but I will not
die, knowing nothing of love. I will be born again to
find her.

IDA: Here's a penny! Sing him a song! No fucking
whatsaname!

LAURIE: Religiosity.

IDA: He's Norfolk. Let's have a song of the country!

*The HANGMAN puts a sack over his head, and slings the noose
round his neck.*

'Pleasant and Delightful' – traditional

STREET SINGER: It was pleasant and delightful one
      midsummer's morn
To see the green fields all covered with corn
And the blackbirds and thrushes sang on
      every green spray
And the larks they sang melodious at the
      dawning of the day

ALL: And the larks they sang melodious
And the larks they sang melodious
And the larks they sang melodious at the
      dawning of the day

OFFICIAL: Daniel James Ross born of Corpusty, near
Saxthorpe, Norfolk.

*DANNY is pushed off the cart, and the Tyburn jig commences. In
silence.*

END OF ACT.

Act Two

DANNY is still twitching on the rope. Enter MARY HOULIHAN (same actress as CAMILLE). She is nine months pregnant.

MARY: Agh feck! Me feet feel wore out, and looking like I done walked from Galway itself. And what a fecking pilgrimage! But the Houlihans are here, and we're all still breathing and dere's only da fecking fairies and Patrick hisself knows how we done it. Aye.

Silence, the crowd watch her.

HUGO: Excuse me miss. Are you Irish?

MARY: I am so. Is this London?

HUGO: Yes.

MARY: Have you seen me cousin Michael?

During the song the HOULIHAN family arrive consisting of MARY's brother PATRICK, his wife, a sow, and many children.

Song: Aaaargh Pat!

Mary: (*Singing.*)   We had a farm in Galway
                No bigger than a garden
                But the taties got afflicted
                So we walked the road to Dublin
                I dream't to go to New York
                But six pounds I could na raise
                A shilling to London and sit on deck
                And fecking freezing all the way.

Enter IRISH, singing. They all go into the one house which we see filling up with pigs, children, etc.

                Aaaargh! Pat!
                Won't you come away!
                Come, come away my butty!
                To live this poor I can't endure

And death is drawing near.
To London!
Come! Come away my dear!

In the pub.

IDA: Fucking Micks! Why – if one Mick wants to say
something to another Mick – why can't he just say it. Why
do they have to get pissed, beat each other up, and then
write a fucking song about it?

LAURIE: Because Irish is an oral culture.

RENNIE: You can't have two religions in one country boy!

IDA: Protestant and Catholic. They're like chalk and
whatsaname –

LAURIE: Cheese.

Enter HUGO and BENNY.

BENNY: Mum, quick, Gaskin's filling nan's house wi' Micks!

IDA: No!

IDA, BENNY and HUGO leave.

RENNIE: I got Irish upstairs from me boy, they got a pig in the
house!

LAURIE: Three in one your pig. Heating, entertainment, and
telling the time.

*IDA is banging on the door where the HOULIHANS have gone in.
HUGO and BENNY watch.*

HUGO: Hundreds of Micks in there Ida, just walked in the
door!

IDA: Get outa there! This is French housing!

A pig comes to the window and looks out.

BENNY: Yeah, we built it mate.

HUGO: One on one, the Micks, they're fucking nothing!

ALBERT GASKIN arrives, dressed in a smart suit, a businessman.

IDA: Oi. Gaskin! These Micks have broken into me old muvver's house!

HUGO: They've got a pig in there Mr Gaskin!

GASKIN: Do you have a loom to go to Mister Bosanquet? (*Rent book in hand.*) Ida…your old 'muvver' –

IDA: – Veronica Popineau.

GASKIN: – died last week. Owing rent.

IDA: She died Sat'day wiv nofin owing, and a new week starts on a Sunday. So I'd say her timing 'vis à vis' the rent was perfect.

GASKIN: You buried her Thursday. She *occupied* the parlour for five days.

IDA: She was fucking dead!

GASKIN: Two shillings 'storage'.

IDA: You promised this house to my Benny, he's got a girl up the whatsaname.

GASKIN: Duff?

IDA: Na, up the Roman Road, they're getting wed.

GASKIN: These rooms have gone to the Houlihan families.

IDA: Rooms? That's an house.

GASKIN: Each family gets a room each.

IDA: You're nofin but an house farmer! Where are we supposed to live?

GASKIN: Florent and his family have gone to Redbridge.

IDA: Redbridge? Never heard of it.

IDA leaves and goes back to the pub.

BENNY: You're not giving them jobs are you Gaskin?

GASKIN: England is a free country.

HUGO: They ain't done their Guild apprenticeships.

GASKIN: The Irish are the finest weavers in Christendom.

BENNY: 'Cheapest' you mean.

In the pub. Enter IDA.

IDA: Gaskin's gone and given me mum's house to a family of Micks!

RENNIE: They're all French houses them!

IDA: Gaskin's great grandfather'll be turning in his grave. He didn't paddle across the Channel in a fucking apple barrel to build houses for the Irish?!

LAURIE: I reckon them barrel stories are a bit exaggerated.

RENNIE: The rivers of London will run with blood boy!

LAURIE: Ses here there's illegal mass houses all over London.

RENNIE: Going on right under our noses boy!

IDA: Foreign priests are filling the heads of these Irish with the madness of Papism!

Enter FATHER CARLO with a loaf of bread, and a Caravaggio painting. He is an Italian priest, but not wearing priestly clothes at this point. He is played by the boy lover.

RENNIE: Should be illegal!

LAURIE: Yet the King's pushing through his Relief Act to tolerate Catholicism.

RENNIE: Spain! France! Rome! This will be war!

CARLO: Buon giorno!

IDA: Ciao Carlo love!

CARLO: How are you this day Mister Laurie?

LAURIE: Cosi, cosi! Grazi, for asking. The usual?

LAURIE hands over the bottle of red. CARLO pays, and LAURIE gives him the keys.

CARLO: Grazi!

CARLO slinks off to the function room where he dresses as a priest.

RENNIE: He's a Catholic priest! You got communion going on up them stairs!

IDA: Carlo? He runs an art appreciation class.

RENNIE: With a loaf of bread and a bottle of red wine!

LAURIE: Today'll be the still life. Table, bread, bottle of red.

IDA: You see a lot of shit like that.

RENNIE: The wine is the blood of Christ, bread is the body of Christ!

LAURIE: O'course! That's how them paintings work on a metaphorical level.

RENNIE: He's ramming Papism down the throats of the Irish under your roof boy!

LAURIE: You're wrong about these country Irish. They're not Catholic. I'll bet you a shilling none of them even heard of the Pope.

RENNIE: The Irish not Catholic?! Two shillings! You're on boy!

LAURIE: Right, let's go find an Irishman.

RENNIE and LAURIE leave the pub. Enter to the street, JOHN and ANNE O'NEILL. A boy with a barrow carries their substantial chests/cases. As they arrive two of the HOULIHAN brothers tumble into the street fighting. MARY follows them out.

HOULIHAN 1: Feck off, that's my stick!

HOULIHAN 2: No, it's my stick, so it is.

MARY: Fight in the street, will yer now! I'm trying to fecking give birth in there!

ANNE: The Irish that give the Irish a bad name are here, before us John.

JOHN: Aye, we'll have to grin and bear it as usual.

ANNE: Did you see that girl, no more than a child and already the devil's had her.

JOHN: There is no devil.

ANNE: You know what I mean, drink, lust, and ignorance.

BARROW BOY: Him there, that's Mr Gaskin.

JOHN: John O'Neill, my wife Anne. You got my letters?

GASKIN: Mr O'Neill, a pleasure. Madame, enchanté. A good journey?

ANNE: It was thrilling, sailing up the Thames, so exciting!

GASKIN: Your room is this way. Far from the common Irish. Where's your pig?

JOHN: I'm a publisher of Philosophical pamphlets.

GASKIN: Forgive me. I thought it was a cultural thing, most of the Irish –

ANNE: – Sir! We don't have a pig.

The O'NEILLS go into their house. RENNIE and LAURIE stand outside the HOULIHANS.

LAURIE: Don't knock! I've heard knocking is rude in their culture.

RENNIE: How can knocking be rude?

LAURIE: The English soldiers used to knock on their doors just before they burned their houses down. 'Knocking' and 'burning down' became connected.

They enter without knocking. PATRICK is having sex with his wife, MARY is giving birth.

MARY: Did yer not think to knock?! We're busy? I'm giving birth and me brother Patrick here is forcing himself on his wife against her will.

LAURIE: We won't keep you. Patrick, have you ever heard of the Pope?

PATRICK: The Pope!? Aye, yes, yes, the Pope, aye, yes I have, aye.

RENNIE: Ha, ha! Two shillings please, Laurie my man!

LAURIE: What do you know about the Pope?

PATRICK: I've heard say, she's a fine powerful beast for a three year old.

LAURIE: Yes!

RENNIE: You think the Pope is a horse!?

PATRICK: Ain't she the filly what won on the sands there at Omey Island?

LAURIE: Two shillings Rennie, thank you. No rush.

LAURIE hands over two shillings to RENNIE. At that moment MARY gives birth with a wail. PATRICK climbs off his wife to take a look at the baby.

MARY: What the feck do you think you're looking at?

PATRICK: Looking at me babby! I am the father ain't I!

LAURIE: Congratulations. We'll be going!

PATRICK: Agh, feck!

CATHERINE: Be Jaysus!

LAURIE: Lord save us! The baby's only got the one eye!

MARY: Sure, the other one'll come through in a bit!

PATRICK: Ah, it's another fecking freak. Get rid of it will yer now!

RENNIE: See you later!

LAURIE and RENNIE leave passing CARLO in the doorway.

LAURIE: Alright Carlo?

CARLO: The Irish, they are all wonderful painters. (*To the HOULIHANS.*) Buon giorno!

MARY: Who are you? The feckin' King of England?

LOVERS' MUSICAL STING.

CARLO: Father Carlo. I can offer you Mass? You are Irish? You belong to Rome?

PATRICK: No! We're from Galway!

CARLO: Agh! The bambino has one eye, in the middle, like the devil!

MARY: You're a 'glass half empty' kinda fella then, Father Carlo!

CARLO: Who is the father?

MARY: Me brother, Patrick, there, him.

CARLO: Your brother is the father!? You must know that it is wrong to make-a sexual intercourse with your own brother.

MARY: Well, Carlo, on that one, we'll have to agree to disagree.

CARLO: Do all your family, make love with each other?

PATRICK: Oh aye, yes, me auld mother brought us up right and proper, aye.

MARY: 'Don't sleep with strangers, it's dirty!' she'd say.

KATHLEEN: 'Keep it in the family, least yer know they've been!' That's one of hers!

CARLO: Sta Migna! Sei pazzo! And you such a sweet little ragazza!

MARY: Ah feck off Carlo! You're a right one for the ladies eh?

CARLO: You must come to mass, the room over the Britannia pub there. I will try and save your soul. Ask for the art appreciation class.

CARLO leaves. In the street. LAURIE and RENNIE talk to HUGO and BENNY. LORD GEORGE GORDON and retinue arrive.

LORD GEORGE: Here! We'll create a Courtyard Theatre in the Shakespearean tradition!

BLACKAMOOR: Coffee! Knockyerblockoffcoffee!

EELS: Live eels! Get yer eels!

LAURIE: I'm telling you this Irish girl, she's given birth to a one eyed baby.

HUGO: Boy or girl?

RENNIE: It doesn't matter boy! It's a monster.

BENNY: Watch your backs!

LORD GEORGE: (*To the crowd.*) Monsieurs dames! Mes amis!

SEA COALS: Sea coals! Open your hatches! Sea coals!

LORD GEORGE: J'arrive aujourd'hui –

BENNY: – we speak English!

HUGO: – nutter!

LORD GEORGE: I have brought my petition to Bethnal Green –

SAUSAGES: – sizzling sausages!

LORD GEORGE: – home of the most industrious, the most creative citizens of England, the French, the survivors of the Saint Bartholomew's Day massacre –

LAURIE: – What do you do then?

LORD GEORGE: I am Lord George Gordon. I am a 'Member of Parliament'.

SEA COALS: So that's what they look like is it?!

LORD GEORGE: – Today I exhort you to rise up against an act of evil which the King has designed to appease the Whore of Babylon, the Pope.

HUGO: I like your trousers!

LORD GEORGE: – the Catholic Relief Act will ease into the vulnerable body corporate of England the soul-deceiving and all-enslaving superstitions of the Witch of Rome. This will not be a door opening to Papism, it will be the walls collapsing, allowing the sewers of Rome to corrupt, disease, and violate, with violation 'pon violation the constitution of we free men. Twenty thousand Irish Catholic terrorists are organising in secret Mass Houses –

BENNY: – An Irish one eyed child has been born in this very street!

LORD GEORGE: Proof that the devil is at work under our noses!

HUGO: Let's kill the monster!

BENNY: Not yet, I wanna hear what he has to say.

LORD GEORGE: Preachers of Hate are twisting Irish minds against us, us! Their hosts! Today I ask you to do two things: sign my petition against the Catholic Relief Act; wear a blue cockade in your hats; and march with me –

BENNY: – that's three things!

LORD GEORGE: Let us march against the House of Commons!
NO POPERY!

HUGO: No Irish?

LORD GEORGE: No Irish!

ALL: NO POPERY! NO IRISH! NO POPERY!

The MOB move off chanting. CARLO works his way back into the pub.

RENNIE: One eye! Smack bang in the middle of the forehead.

IDA: How many legs?

LAURIE: Two I think.

IDA: Cloven feet?

In the pub, enter JOHN and ANNE O'NEILL.

JOHN: A glass of beer please, and my wife would like a port.

IDA: Can't you bleedin' read!?

JOHN: Your 'No Blacks, No Irish, No Dogs' notice in the window?

ANNE: (*Pointing at RENNIE.*) What about him?

IDA: Rennie?

LAURIE: He's not Irish.

ANNE: Do you judge a nation by its worst ambassadors?

IDA: Course!

ANNE: If I were to run an inn I would ban individuals for their behaviour, their nationality would be irrelevant.

IDA: Get yourself a pub then lady, run it like a fucking brothel, see how long you last!

RENNIE: Are you Catholics?

ANNE: No. Not all the Irish are for Rome. Or drunk. Or poor.

JOHN: I'm a publisher. I publish pamphlets on the Enlightenment.

LAURIE: You doubt the resurrection of Christ don't you?

ANNE: We raise questions of Epistemology.

IDA: He pissed 'em all off, that's why they crucified him!

JOHN: What is the logic of not serving a gentleman whose money is as good as any Englishman's?

IDA: It's a free country! I'm allowed to be fucking illogical!

ANNE: What a shame.

JOHN: You see, I am a member of the Humanist Society. The secretary has asked me to find a room in the East End where we can hold regular meetings.

ANNE: Three hundred steady drinking atheists.

LAURIE: The room's free of a Wednesday, after art appreciation. Ida?

IDA: Pint and a port!?

MARY with baby runs into the pub.

MARY: Where is he? Please! Carlo!? Art appreciation?

IDA: Up them apples!

MARY runs upstairs with the baby.

ANNE: She's had the baby then?

LAURIE: Yeah, it's got one eye, it's a right proper Cyclops.

RENNIE: You're looking at the work of the devil!

ANNE: There is no devil sir. That child is the product of poverty and ignorance.

MARY bursts into the function room.

MARY: Carlo!

CARLO: Mary! You have come!

MARY: Patrick wants to kill me babby!

CARLO: You are safe here with me. Mary, can you feel a connection, a timeless bond with me? Do you feel it?

MARY: I've just given birth. I can't feel a fecking thing. You should try it!

CARLO: But did you hear the music when we first met?

MARY: Aye, I heard it. It'll be the fairies. They've had it in for me ever since I stood on one of the little fellahs. My punishment for that accident is bleeding, regular, every month, from a place you wouldn't believe.

CARLO: We know each other, somehow, the Lord has brought me to London, brought you to London, to meet, to fulfil some greater purpose.

MARY: Ah! What a helluva line of chat, you're a regular charmer eh!

He holds her tight and clumsy.

CARLO: Oh! To hold you, to feel you! I know now what my life is for!

He tries to kiss, but she stops him.

MARY: So this is mass is it!? You'll be cracking open a bottle next! Stop! We can't kiss.

CARLO: Why not?!

MARY: You're not even a friend of the family.

CARLO collapses to his knees holding MARY's legs. Enter LAURIE, JOHN and ANNE.

LAURIE: Don't mind us Carlo, just showing the room.

CARLO jumps up, adjusts his tackle, and picks up the picture. It is the Caravaggio.

CARLO: Appreciate the art, here, Thomas frowns as he sticks a finger in Christ's wounds. Appreciate how Carravaggio shows *doubt* as a contagion!

JOHN: What I appreciate is how Caravaggio presents doubt as a human obligation.

ANNE: The 'frown' is the mother of The Enlightenment.

MARY: You sound like Jackeens from Dublin!?

ANNE: We're Irish, yes, Bray town, and publishers.

JOHN: We have said 'no thank you' to the supernatural.

The baby cries.

ANNE: Oh, what a beautiful baby! She's got her mother's eye.

CARLO: It's a punishment from God for incest!

JOHN: God has no hand in this. A deformed child is a consequence of nature.

LAURIE: What if God's intelligence designed nature? The deformed baby is then simultaneously a consequence of nature, *and* a punishment from God. Publish that mate.

In the street, the MOB, inflamed, carrying torches. LAURIE goes to the window.

MOB: NO POPERY! NO IRISH! NO POPERY!

LAURIE: They're killing Catholics. They're burning your brother's house.

HUGO: Give us the one eyed devil child!

LAURIE: They want the baby.

LAURIE exits.

MOB: Kill, Kill, Kill! (*And under through the next section.*)

CARLO: They're coming this way. Hide the bambino!

MARY hides the baby in a draw/box/cupboard.

BENNY: Throw the monster out or we'll burn you down!

JOHN: If we had any kind of monster we'd give her up to you now!

MOB: Irish! In the pub! Burn the pub!

BENNY: Fuck off! That's a decent pub!

CARLO: They're coming in, swords drawn.

RENNIE enters, ushering in HUGO and BENNY both with swords drawn.

RENNIE: I'm telling you, him there, he's a priest, and these two are Irish.

JOHN: We're Irish yes, but we're not Catholic.

ANNE: We're intellectuals from Wicklow.

HUGO: Where's your one eyed baby?

MARY: I'll not tell you. You'll have to kill me first!

HUGO grabs CARLO and puts a sword to his heart. BENNY keeps the O'NEILLS at bay with his sword.

HUGO: Cough up love! Or I'll run him through.

BENNY: I know him. He will!

CARLO: Don't tell them Mary!

MARY: She's not a monster, she's my little babby so!

HUGO thrusts his sword into CARLO. CARLO collapses, dying.

CARLO: Mary, my sweet, I am dying, I will see you in paradise.

JOHN: Maybe it's not the time to disappoint you father, but reason alone tells us that there is no heaven, and there's no hell neither.

ANNE: This is the only paradise you will ever know.

CARLO: Bethnal Green?

JOHN: Aye. It's a sobering thought isn't it.

CARLO dies. The baby cries giving away the location. HUGO lifts the lid.

HUGO: I'm telling you mate, that is the anti-christ and no mistaking.

BENNY holds MARY back with his sword. HUGO picks the baby up and takes it to the window where he shows his trophy to the crowd.

Here you go! I got the Catholic devil child!

HUGO throws the child out of the window. The doll/baby lands on the stage. The audience should see it land and be shocked with the texture of its bounce. Enter SCHIMMEL and family. Jews from the Pale.

SCHIMMEL: Oy gevalt! Did you see that! And you think it's tough being Jewish!

END OF ACT.

Act Three

1888. Continue from the last scene, the mob turn and watch the Jewish refugees arrive.

STREET SINGER: Behold! what beasts come wailing through
          the lock?
          On cattle ships to Saint Katherine's dock
          A human invasion of an alien variation
          The children of the He-brew Nation
          The Eternal People, oppressed, ground down
          A Shtetl to make of our tenter ground
          This swarming is the most unwelcome news
          For the French, the Irish. And the
             English... Jews

The docks. The sound of a ship's horn, deep and mournful. Enter the elite of Anglo Jewry: CHIEF RABBI, LORD ROTHSCHILD and MP HARRY SAMUELS.

RABBI: Look at all these Luftmensch!

HARRY: Don't they say Chief Rabbi, 'one gets the Jews one deserves'.

RABBI: Hell, I must have killed in my sleep!

ROTHSCHILD: I must build them a synagogue.

RABBI: And quickly please Lord Rothschild! Or they will come to mine!

ROTHSCHILD: They're hungry.

RABBI: Yes, but quiet! Feed them, they'll start arguing!

ROTHSCHILD: Harry? This is your constituency, would a temporary shelter be possible? Food, a doctor, clothing and –

RABBI: – a Klezmer band!

HARRY: If we make it too easy for them, more will come.

RABBI: 'Dear Uncle Heime, sell the cow, come to London, there is a free meal.' Starvation is our best weapon!

HARRY: And we should tell them about South Africa.

RABBI: Yes, how wonderful it is!

ROTHSCHILD: Is it wonderful?

HARRY: Who cares! It's somewhere else!

ROTHSCHILD: We have to help. These are our people. What would Moses do?

RABBI: Moses would not be here. He'd be in New York already!

ROTHSCHILD: They need housing, hospitals, schools. Our mission is to turn these Jews into English Jews.

KATZ arrives, and starts selling the paper.

KATZ: Spread *The Revolution*!

HARRY: Anarchists.

KATZ: Support the Jewish Anarchist League!

ROTHSCHILD: *Jewish* anarchists! Is that possible?

RABBI: Apparently, there are many terrorists on these ships. Army deserters.

ROTHSCHILD: Chief Rabbi? Have you been dining at the Russian Embassy again?

RABBI: I have to eat!

Enter BLACK RUTH. She rather ostentatiously kisses KATZ, then starts selling the paper.

RUTH: You may join the Jewish Anarchist League here! Fight the awful business of international capital.

ROTHSCHILD: Good Lord, I recognise her.

KATZ and RUTH kiss again.

RABBI: I've heard these anarchists will sleep with anybody.

ROTHSCHILD: Are they Libertarians?

RABBI: God knows what they eat!

RUTH: Wouldn't it be fun to destroy marriage, religion, and chastity!

ROTHSCHILD: My God! It's Ruth, Tufty's daughter. Excuse me gentlemen.

ROTHSCHILD approaches RUTH.

RUTH: Lord Rothschild?

ROTHSCHILD: Ruth?

RUTH: Black Ruth.

ROTHSCHILD: What are you doing here?

RUTH: I'm organising a revolution, kicking off with a terrific dock strike.

ROTHSCHILD: At your own father's docks?

RUTH: Indeedy! Next a tailors' strike. Imagine, the Jewish tailors and the Irish dockers, united! I've organised a walk.

KATZ: March.

RUTH: A *march* to Parliament. Oh fuckioli! It's father! Spread the Revolution!

Enter LORD BALLAST, he sees RUTH and steams. He is a bald headed man with tufty red eyebrows. He is wearing a Rolls Royce of a coat.

ROTHSCHILD: Tufty! Have you seen your daughter, Ruth.

TUFTY: Oh buggerello, is she here again!? Excuse me gentlemen!

TUFTY goes over to RUTH.

Ruth! What's this bloody rag you're selling?

RUTH: *The Revolution.* A shilling.

TUFTY: It says here a penny.

RUTH: It's a shilling to you.

He pays for a paper, and gives it a quick scan.

Father, how many workers died stitching that coat?

TUFTY: Four. The typesetting is ruddy awful. 'The Jewish
  Anarchist League meets on the *sixty sixth* of September.'

RUTH: Oh cock au vin!

TUFTY: If a thing's worth doing, it's worth doing well!

He turns his back on her, and walks back to ROTHSCHILD.

Children eh? I should've stuck to breeding horses.
  Gentlemen! Welcome to my big dock!

ROTHSCHILD: Lord Ballast, the Chief Rabbi, and you know
  the MP, Harry Samuel.

TUFTY: Always, nice, to add more Jewish friends to the
  collection! So, you can see, thousands of these aliens are
  coming in every week. Criminals, anarchists, terrorists, and
  the odd religious nutter! Ha!

He slaps the RABBI on the back.

HARRY: The most pressing –

TUFTY: – I've had an idea. What if you Jews had your own
  country!?

RABBI: A homeland for the Jews would be –

TUFTY: – Have you ever considered Palestine?! Palestine is
  a country without a people, and the Jews, are a people
  without a country.

HARRY: – there are many Arabs and –

TUFTY: – AND the good news is the Ottoman Empire is about to go tits up, and Johnny Turk'll sell his own mother in a closing down sale!

KATZ: Spread the Revolution!

TUFTY: Half of these yid…dish speaking refugees are intent on destroying our way of life. Do you want to talk to one? Hey, you! Come here!

AARON comes over.

ROTHSCHILD: Shalom aleichem!

AARON: Shalom!

HARRY: How do you expect to survive in this town young man?

AARON: I am a printer.

TUFTY: Typesetting?

AARON: I can typeset, yes. My brother is here, and he says there are many newspapers in New York?

ROTHSCHILD: This is London.

AARON: No! The captain said it was New York!

TUFTY: You're not the first. (*To the gents.*) Come on let's go and eat!

The committee move off. TUFTY turns and approaches AARON. He slips him some money.

Hey! My card. Come and see me tomorrow. If you're looking for employment, they need a typesetter.

TUFTY exits. AARON approaches RUTH.

RUTH: Comrade! Take a paper. It's yours.

AARON takes the paper and the LOVERS MUSICAL STING PLAYS. RUTH is affected by the music, almost swooning. AARON is unmoved.

AARON: This typesetting's awful. I can typeset.

In the pub.

IDA: Fucking Yids! Ain't they never heard of soap and wa'er!? Last time any of this lot had a bath was two thousand years ago in the River Jordan. In the whole wide world is there one other whatsaname –

LAURIE: – independent civilised nation state –

IDA: – what is willing to take the scrapings of Russia, Poland, no questions asked.

RENNIE: I got them upstairs from me, fish for breakfast, fish for lunch, fish for tea!

LAURIE: There's no smoke without salmon with this lot.

RENNIE: Britain got an open door boy!

IDA: Why is it so fucking difficult to ask the odd question? Like, 'have you got smallpox?' 'Have you got cholera?'

LAURIE: 'Did you assassinate Tsar Alexander the second?'

The revolutionaries' flat in Whitechapel. RUTH, KATZ, AARON. A bed, and a printing press.

AARON: Aaron Biro, St Petersburg.

KATZ: Martin Katz, Bellozersk.

RUTH: Black Ruth, Stow-on-the-Wold. I'm cooking a peasant style paella, and there's plenty of vin de table.

AARON: In Russia I was earning seven roubles a week for typesetting and layout.

KATZ: We don't pay wages.

RUTH: On principle. Wages, you see, are chains. But you can sleep with me – if you want. There are no rules, you don't have to.

KATZ: Marriage is the institutionalised oppression of women.

RUTH: We're libertarians. Martin, go next door and ask Mrs T if we can borrow that spare mattress of hers. For you.

KATZ leaves, sulky.

Aaron, did you hear the music, at the docks, when we met?

AARON: I didn't hear anything. I suffer from tinnitis. From the printing presses.

RUTH: I was powerless. I felt watched, as if Cupid was taking aim.

AARON: Why are you using the standard nine point Clarendon upright? The layout is aggressively homogeneous. Do you have a set of nine point Bulmer italic?

RUTH: What are you talking about?

AARON: Printing. I love all aspects of printing but fonts are my real passion.

RUTH: Oh dear. Really?

AARON: Yes, I have invented a portable pen.

AARON takes out what looks like a narrow steel tube. It is his prototype ball point pen.

It has a rotating ball in a steel coated socket.

RUTH: Mister Aaron Biro, you're a clever cloggs aren't you!

She takes his hand and their two hands write with the biro.

It's beautiful, and functional, like you. Have you got a name for it?

AARON: I call it the 'Stahlmantel-kugel-in-tinte-mit-muffe'.

RUTH: Holy fuckioli! That's a mouthful!

AARON: People shorten it to –

She kisses him.

RUTH: – I should find you dull, and cerebral, but I can't resist you.

Enter KATZ, carrying mattress. He stands and watches.

We were discussing the next issue of *The Revolution*. It must include our 'God, and the dinosaurs' polemic.

KATZ: Why, if God made dinosaurs are they not mentioned in the Bible?

AARON: You could say the same about a round earth, bacteria, the circulation of the blood – the list is endless.

RUTH: Martin, we have discovered a great mind! The essay must be rewritten! I will sit with Aaron as he typesets. You can sleep in the scullery.

MARTIN KATZ exits with the mattress. AARON is at the press, and RUTH snuggles in beside him.

RUTH: We can make love all night now.

She kisses him.

AARON: My plan is to join my brother in New York and develop the pen for the American market. I need paid work so that I can save for my fare.

RUTH: You can look for enslavement tomorrow, Mister Biro, tonight you're free.

AARON: What kind of work is available for a Jew in London?

Lights down on the flat and lights up on the sweatshop.

Song: 'Oy vey!'

> Hard and bitter as death is this life
> Oy vey! Oy vey!
> All my strength for a crust for my wife
> Oy vey! Oy vey!
> The Sweater here he is a Jew
> Oy vey! Oy Vey!
> Hoffman and Singer they were too!

Oy vey! Oy vey! Oy vey! Oy vey!

Enter LAZARUS, the sweater, and AARON.

LAZARUS: I will train you and then you will be able to earn twenty shillings a week.

AARON: You will pay me twenty shillings a week?

LAZARUS: When I have trained you, you will be able to earn twenty shillings a week.

AARON: Somewhere else?

LAZARUS: I am training you for life. You should be paying me. Take it or leave it.

> We all wish for death every day!
> Oy vey! Oy vey!
> Heat and steam we can't get away
> Oy vey! Oy vey!
> The Factory Act's kept out of sight
> Oy vey! Oy vey!
> We stop for God on a Friday night
> Oy vey! Oy vey! Oy vey! Oy vey!

AARON looks at TUFTY's card and leaves. MRS GASKIN kicks out the Irish.

MRS GASKIN: Come on! Let's be having you! Chop! Chop!

IDA: Oi! Mrs Gaskin, what the fuck are you doing?! These is Irish houses.

MRS GASKIN: My great great great grandfather didn't paddle across the English Channel in an apple barrel because he wanted advice from the likes of you.

IDA: You promised number sixteen to my girl!

MRS GASKIN: No Christians need apply.

HUGO: The yids wanna be near the sweatshops innit.

Enter RABBI. He shakes hands with MRS GASKIN.

MRS GASKIN: Morning Rabbi, turned out nice again!

RABBI: Yes, yes, I've got the money.

HUGO: Oi Mrs Gaskin, what you selling him?

MRS GASKIN hands over a big church key.

BENNY: You can't sell the church!

HUGO: Gaskin's selling the French church!

The RABBI disposes of the cross on the outside of the church and puts up a star of David.

BENNY: We ain't gonna stand for a synagogue round here Mrs Gaskin.

MRS GASKIN: Move then. It's a free country.

IDA: Where are we Irish supposed to go then?

MRS GASKIN: I've heard Redbridge is very nice.

IDA: Redbridge? I wouldn't be seen fucking dead in Redbridge!

TUFTY sits at his office desk. A SECRETARY enters.

SECRETARY: The minutes of the red squirrel society sir. And there is an alien to see you. He produced your card.

TUFTY: Send him in.

Enter AARON.

Did you find accommodation?

AARON: The Flower and Dean Street rookery.

TUFTY: Neighbors with Jack the Ripper! My theory is that Jack is a kosher butcher.

AARON: He is as likely to be an English gentleman.

TUFTY: Employment?

AARON: I'm typesetting *The Revolution*, and looking for paid work.

TUFTY: What do you want from life Aaron Biro?

AARON: Until last night I had wanted my pen to change the world but –

TUFTY: – another bloody writer eh?

AARON: Inventor. This is my portable pen. The 'Stahlmantel-kugel-in-tinte-mit-muffe'. Everybody shortens it to 'mitmuffe'.

TUFTY: 'Mitmuffe'? As in 'would you like to borrow my mitmuffe'?

AARON: Yes.

TUFTY: I wouldn't buy one because I'm prejudiced against anything German or German sounding.

TUFTY gets out some money and puts it on the table.

Change the typesetting from 'spread The Revolution' to 'destroy The Revolution' and I will give you fifteen pounds. Your ticket to New York.

AARON: Why does that concern you so much?

TUFTY: They're organising the Irish, the dockers, to strike. I own the docks.

AARON: I cannot help. I have chosen to stay in England. I've met a girl.

TUFTY: This girl, is she a well bred aristocratic Englishwoman?

AARON: Yes.

TUFTY: (*Stands.*) Holy moly buggeroli! Thirty pounds! Fifteen for your fare and fifteen to get you started in America with your mitmuffe!

AARON: No. I adore her.

TUFTY: Mister Biro, I could have you arrested for rape. Ruthey is my only daughter, and will in time recover her station. She will not marry a hairy Jew with no prospects! Fifty pounds!

AARON: I cannot be bought.

AARON makes to leave.

TUFTY: The offer stands! Any time!

TUFTY sits head in hands, distraught. A graffiti artist paints ENGLAND FOR THE ENGLISH on the synagogue wall. A banner proclaims THE BRITISH BROTHERS LEAGUE.

MOB: England for the English!
England for the English!
England for the English!

HARRY SAMUEL: I, Harry Samuel, have never put my religion, my Jewishness, ahead of my duties as your MP. That is why today I welcome to the East End the British Brothers League and their inspiration, Major Evans-Gordon!

Cheers.

MAJOR EG: Roman, Viking, Saxon, French, and Irish – all have integrated successfully, and with God's genius, created the Englishman. But a Hebrew can only marry a Hebrew, the synagogue is separative!

WOMAN: My boy is the only Christian in his 'ole school!

MAJOR EG: And what do they bring with them?

BENNY: Jack the Ripper!

HUGO: Jacob the Ripper!

Laughter.

MAJOR EG: If we don't act now this is the end of England! Join the British Brothers League, and we will close the door on this foul ingress of humanity!

Cheers. The flat. RUTH is there, and TUFTY. He stands, exasperated at the squalor.

TUFTY: Living here! With a Jew! What could be worse?

RUTH: Two Jews?

TUFTY: Holy moly fuckioli! Come home please! The servants miss you terribly!

RUTH: I have vital work here in Bethnal Green.

TUFTY: I spent an hour last week begging the Duke of Bedford not to introduce the American grey squirrel into Woburn Park. The British squirrel will stand no chance against this voracious, sexually charged, immigrant! Why Ruthey!? Why this lust for Hebrew flesh?!

RUTH: Mother told me that as a deb she was very fond of a Sassoon or two.

TUFTY: I'll get them a country of their own if it's the last thing I do, and with a bit of luck they'll all go and live there. It will bring peace to the world.

TUFTY starts to leave as the Jewish Anarchist League members arrive for their meeting. AARON and others arrive. They all tuck in to the food. The feeling is not revolutionary but convivial.

MORRIE: I've got chola, still warm, gefilte fish, pickled –

AARON: – excellent Morrie!

Enter KATZ with HUGO. HUGO looks a bit sceptical, lost, embarrassed.

MORRIE: I read your essay Mister Katz. It's the most comprehensive anarcho-communist analysis of capitalism I've ever read in Yiddish.

RUTH kisses AARON. KATZ approaches RUTH and takes her to one side.

KATZ: I have found you an Irish docker.

RUTH: Oh goodo!

KATZ: A tailors' and dockers' strike would do two things. It would break the barriers of racial antipathy between Jews and Irish and –

RUTH: – and it'll give Parliament and daddy a well deserved bloody nose.

KATZ: I'm relying on you Ruth. You have to deliver. Sleep with him.

KATZ moves away. RUTH is left thoughtful.

AARON: Does Katz love you?

RUTH: He has made love to me.

AARON: Don't torture me! I was a printer, an inventor, living entirely in my head until last night.

RUTH: Love is the invention of the oppressed sprung from the well of economic misery.

KATZ brings HUGO over to RUTH. AARON defers and backs away, and watches.

KATZ: This is Hugo. Black Ruth. One of the girls I was telling you about.

HUGO: Awight! Your china's been telling me you're one of them Libertarians.

RUTH: Indeed I am. Are the dockers organised?

HUGO: No. Most of us are married.

MORRIE claps his hands to start the meeting.

MORRIE: Shalom Aleichem! Sit down, sit down! Comrades! Chaverim! Quiet! First the minutes of the Jewish Anarchist League for –

AARON: – We must change our name! How can one be a Jewish anarchist! An anarchist rejects all authority, all religion, and reaches out to any and every worker. A Jew defers to a higher authority.

MORRIE: 'Jewish' is only an adjective, it means 'friendly, clean, well organised'.

KATZ: I am a 'Jewish anarchist' and I like these meetings, they're…they're –

MORRIE: – heimische!

AARON: But to be a Jew is to be particular.

MORRIE: Particular about everything! Milk and meat, washing –

AARON: – the meeting should be open to Christians, Hindus, Mohammadans.

MORRIE: You can do the catering!

RUTH: Tchisikov, are you an anarchist or a Jewish anarchist?

TCHISIKOV: I love death.

LILLY: In the pogroms they massacre Jews, not workers. Jews must reach inside, into their traditions.

KATZ: So you are the Orthodox Jewish Anarchist League!

LILLY: Throw stones, that's easy! Why not take those stones and build a nation. Israel will be built on anarchist principles.

KATZ: Ah! The Jewish Zionist Anarchist League!

THOMAS: I'm with Aaron. Jews are our worst enemies. Bastard communists like Marx, Engels, Jew capitalists like Rothschild, Montagu –

KATZ: – the anti-semitic Jewish Anarchist League!

RUTH: Chaps! Please! Aaron is right! We should drop Jewish from the name. God is an authoritarian. If I ever meet him I will spit in his eye.

LILLY: You will go to hell.

RUTH: Oh what a lot of cock au vin! There is neither hell nor heaven. This is the only heaven we will ever know.

LILLY: What? Bethnal Green?

RUTH: You could always move darling.

MORRIE: My uncle, he's moved out to this little village. Very quiet. Hendon.

RUTH: We need to find a way of attacking both religion and capital.

MORRIE: On Yom Kippur, I have noticed, the rich gather in the synagogue in seats set aside from the luftmensch.

LILLY: We can do nothing on the Day of Atonement but fast –

AARON: – Instead of fasting we should feast! A bacon sandwich eating competition outside the synagogue!

RUTH: You're a genius Aaron Biro!

TCHISIKOV: (*Standing.*) I love death!

RUTH and TCHISIKOV kiss. Everyone watches. Silence.

HUGO: I can get you some knock off bacon.

MORRIE: Of course! But would it be kosher?!

RUTH: Next meeting, the synagogue on Yom Kippur!

The meeting disperses. TCHISIKOV approaches RUTH.

TCHISIKOV: I am ready. Tomorrow. Aldersgate underground station.

RUTH: Look Tchisy, you don't have to, it was only an idea. Katzie!

KATZ comes over.

Tchisikov says he's ready. Tomorrow. Aldersgate.

KATZ: Did you decide –

TCHISIKOV: – Only suicide can express my love of death!

KATZ hugs TCHISIKOV. TCHISIKOV moves off. KATZ takes RUTH roughly by the arm.

KATZ: (*Bullying.*) If Tchisikov can blow himself up on the underground the least you can do is sleep with a docker.

HUGO comes over with a bit of a swagger. RUTH puts on a brave face.

RUTH: Dockers and tailors marching together will be quite a spectacle.

HUGO: Won't be easy. They've taken our houses, our schools, yer can't move in the hospital for tripping over some Hebrew coughing his guts up.

They start to leave, together. AARON approaches.

RUTH: Come on! I've never seen the docks at night!

AARON: Ruth!

RUTH: I am not impressed by jealousy. Social progress must take priority over –

AARON: – over love!?

RUTH: Yes! You have a night of typesetting. I have my own work.

RUTH and HUGO leave. AARON is distraught.

AARON: Will she sleep with him?

KATZ: Yes. We should put the Yom Kippur polemic on the back page.

AARON: No! The back page banner 'Spread The Revolution' is iconic, and must never be changed.

In the pub. RENNIE, and LAURIE. Enter IDA, taking her coat off.

IDA: Kaw! You can't move out there for yids! I mean, England, ever since the whatsaname –

LAURIE: – disestablishment of the church under Henry the Eighth –

IDA: – has been a Christian country!

LAURIE: Yom Kippur innit. The Day of Atonement.

RENNIE: Your Jew looks to God for absolution from offence.

IDA: That would be a solution, a fence. A fucking big fence round the whole fucking country!

LAURIE is reading. RENNIE is there too.

LAURIE: Your prayers are answered Ida, the Aliens Act got through Parliament.

IDA: 'Bout time too!

RENNIE: England is full boy!

LAURIE: Hang on! Says here, they're still letting them in! Except 'the destitutes, the mad, and the idiots'.

RENNIE: How do they know which ones are the idiots!?

LAURIE: They ask 'em at the docks.

RENNIE: What did you do in Russia?

LAURIE: I was an idiot!

RENNIE: Fuck that! You're not coming in!

LAURIE: Next!

They laugh. The synagogue is packed with observant JEWS. The sound of praying/singing. A Klezmer band are there waiting. Tuning up.

KATZ: Spread The Revolution!

MORRIE: Bacon sandwiches! Get your bacon butties!

RUTH arrives.

RUTH: Where's Aaron? Katzie, tell me! Where is he?!

KATZ: I've not seen him today. Spread The Revolution!

RUTH: Morrie, when did you last see Aaron?

MORRIE: Lunch I had simmus, he had kreplach in chicken soup –

RUTH: – Where is he!?

MORRIE: (*Shrug of the shoulders.*) He had a suitcase.

RUTH: Tchisikov!? Have you seen Aaron?

TCHISIKOV: No.

RUTH: Wait! You were supposed to blow yourself up on the tube?!

TCHISIKOV: One can only really love death if one believes in paradise.

RUTH: So what did you do?

TCHISIKOV: I left the bomb on the train and ran away. Sixty injured, and one dead.

RUTH: What? Someone really died? They're actually dead?

TCHISIKOV: Yes. A capitalist. Spread The Revolution!

RUTH approaches the leader of the klezmer band.

RUTH: Play. What are you waiting for?

MUSICIAN: The bride.

RUTH: This isn't a wedding! Play, and eat these. Bacon sandwiches!

The band play. The RABBI comes out!

RABBI: Oy gevalt! You can't play here! Not today, it is Yom Kippur!

MORRIE: What'll you have Rabbi!? Smoked, streaky or back?

JEW 1: Stop it! You can't eat on Yom Kippur.

JEW 2: They're not just eating, they're eating bacon!

RABBI: Oy a klog! Please stop this, or there will be violence!

The band stop. RUTH stands on a soap box.

RUTH: On your Jewish day of Yom Kippur, I invite you to reject oppression, reject authority, reject God. Eat bacon, dance, and make love!

RABBI: Do not tempt the wrath of the Lord!

RUTH: Lord of the Heavens! I give you ten seconds to destroy me, one, two, three, four, five, six, seven, eight, nine and hello! ten!

The klezmer band break into an up tempo number, and a fight starts. RUTH wrestles free of the situation. A riotous laugh cracks the air. The RABBI holds a copy of The Revolution.

RABBI: Buy a paper, it's so funny! Destroy The Revolution. Look! Destroy The Revolution! The Lord has shown his hand! You are destroyed!

An observant JEW stands on the soap box handing out copies of the paper. Another joins on the second soap box, and then on the third. They are joyful, laughing.

JEW 1: Look! Destroy The Revolution!

JEW 2: Ha, ha! Destroy The Revolution!!

The JEWS drive out the anarchists. RUTH is left alone, distraught. She is crying, wailing, it's desperate, she's on her knees with a copy of the paper.

RUTH: Aaron! My love! Where are you! Have you seen Aaron!? I wanted to tell him. I'm sorry! Aaron! Nothing matters without you!

A Sylheti LASCAR runs on. He approaches RUTH with a bit of cardboard.

LASCAR: Address. Master Attar. Big man barriwallah!

PHILIPPA: Lights! Ginny! Please!

General wash of lights.

What are you doing!?

LASCAR: Have I got something wrong?

PHILIPPA: We're taking an interval before the Bangladeshi act! And we've cut your bit.

POLICEMAN: No-one told me.

PHILIPPA: Everybody, well done, the cockney accents are so authentic.

GINNY: (*Off/distort.*) Thank you everybody! Fifteen minutes. It's all fantastic!

TATYANA: Can I smoke now?

PHILIPPA: Yes please do. And I hope your cigarettes do exactly what they say they do on the tin. (*To herself.*) Kill.

TATYANA walks away. The cast disperse, except TAHER. OFFICER KELLY enters.

OFFICER KELLY: Their envelopes have just arrived. They're here no?

PHILIPPA: Oh shit!

GINNY: (*Off/Distort.*) Shall I give them out?

PHILIPPA: Hell! No, not yet. What is it Taher?

TAHER: Is…

PHILIPPA: – stop! I've warned you, if you mention Israel, that's it!

TAHER: Is –

PHILIPPA: – I mean it!

TAHER: Is this a play about immigration or is it about love?

PHILIPPA: Your point?

TAHER: The play is like four Romeo and Juliets, but what does it matter? I worry, we may have made the play too light, everybody falls in love – in love, out of love, why is it so important?

PHILIPPA: We discussed this during the research. The truest measure of racial and cultural integration in any society is the rate of inter-marriage, and you yourself –

TAHER: – I am agreeing with you! Working on this play I have come to savour the music when the lovers meet. It is the music of hope, humanity.

PHILIPPA: I'm amazed. At last we agree.

TAHER: Yes. Only love can free humanity from the shackles of history. And that is exactly what those bastard Israelis will never understand!

PHILIPPA: Taher, would you, could you, please, just fuck off out of my sight. You're on your INTERVAL!

GINNY: (*Off.*) Fifteen minutes please. Fifteen minutes everybody!

SNAP TO BLACK.

INTERVAL.

Act Four (Prologue)

GINNY: (*Off.*) Act Two beginners to the stage please!

ELMAR is alone on stage. He is joined by TAHER.

TAHER: Our envelopes are in the sound box. They have to give them to us.

ELMAR: In Azerbaydzhan we have a saying, don't kick a sleeping dog, it might wake up and bite your arse.

TAHER: You might have got leave to remain. Or are you expecting bad news?

ELMAR: I told them the truth.

TAHER: Why did you have to leave Azerbaydzhan?

ELMAR: My films, scripted by Aram Magomedli, ridiculed the government's violent suppression of free speech. I felt safe, because there was never anyone in government intelligent enough to understand the metaphor. But last year, my script writer, my friend, Aram Magomedli –

TAHER: – they killed him?

ELMAR: No. He became Minister of Culture.

Enter PHILIPPA.

Your husband is enjoying it I think.

PHILIPPA: I've asked him to sit further back.

ELMAR: That is because you know that this next act includes a portrait of your marriage. St John and Camilla, St John and Philippa?

PHILIPPA: I never expected him to come.

ELMAR: Camilla is a liberal, and you make her an idiot? Are you an idiot? The English tradition is liberal, tolerant. What are you saying?

Enter all the others from outside, TATYANA still smoking.

PHILIPPA: This is a place of work and smoking is illegal! If you want to smoke go back to Serbia where I imagine smoking is still compulsory! I'm not doing notes –

TATYANA: – We have been talking about Deborah.

PHILIPPA: Yes what?

SANYA: She is sixteen years old in the Blitz, yes?

TATYANA: And she gives birth to twins just after 9/11. She is nearly eighty.

PHILIPPA: And the problem is?

SANYA: Physiological!

PHILIPPA: Our characters are children, and their playground is time. One advantage of theatre, over say telecomms, is that one is not bound by reality. Now –

TATYANA: – our envelopes are here.

YAYAH: I want my envelope please.

TATYANA: You don't have the fucking right to keep our envelopes from us. If I have got leave to remain, I can go now!

PHILIPPA: (*Sigh.*) OK. Officer Kelly give the envelopes out please.

ELMAR: No! We have devised this play together. We are a society. Do not destroy that society before we need to. Tatyana, give us one more hour of your life. Then you can have your envelope for ever more.

YAYAH: Good point! I don't want my envelope. I will forget my lines.

PHILIPPA: Thank you, now –

TAHER: – I think there is a problem with Laurie's big speech.

PHILIPPA: (*Dropping her head in resignation.*) Agggh!

TAHER: Laurie is talking about *Pride and Prejudice*, yes? I look on Wikipedia and Elizabeth Bennet loves Fitzwilliam D'Arcy, not Colin Firth.

LAURIE: I have learned my lines now, I am going to say Colin Firth and that is that!

TAHER: But Colin Firth makes no sense –

PHILIPPA: – because it's my English humour not your Gaza Strip humour! Stick with 'Colin Firth'. Thank you. Check your props! House lights! The Blitz! Please!

The lights adjust, and a second world war air raid siren sounds.

Act Four

Summer 1941. The Blitz. An air raid siren. A Bethnal Green street, the Britannia Pub as was. The street of Victorian workers' houses is now overlooked by the Rothschild Buildings. All buildings are blacked out for night and war. In a doorway, Mohammad Sona Rasul aka MISTER MUSHI, beside him a large cooking pot full of clothes, etc. MUSHI is the boy lover. Two wet Bangladeshis run on chased by a policeman, they go off. Enter two STRETCHER BEARERS. They discover a body in a doorway. They are joined by a POLICE CONSTABLE.

CONSTABLE: Indian Lascar. Merchant navy. Stoker? Donkey wallah? Who knows?

STRETCHER BEARER 1: Who cares? He's dead.

CONSTABLE: He'll have jumped ship at Tilbury. They swim the dock.

STRETCHER BEARER 2: Criminal then, ain't he.

CONSTABLE: As a citizen of British India, he has the legal right to come ashore. So come on lads, show some compassion, he's a human soul, and some mother's son.

STRETCHER BEARER 1: You alright officer?

CONSTABLE: I've been on a course.

MUSHI is loaded onto the stretcher. He sneezes/coughs.

STRETCHER 2: That's all we need.

STRETCHER 1: Oi Mush! Hop it!

MUSHI is tipped off the stretcher and the bearers move off to find a corpse.

MUSHI: (*Giving CONSTABLE a bit of cardboard.*) Uncle friend! Big man barriwallah!

CONSTABLE: (*Reading.*) This address is Aldgate.

MUSHI: England people very nice!

CONSTABLE: There's good and bad in all. Come on Mush! This way.

They walk off. In the pub. IDA, LAURIE, and RENNIE. BENNY and HUGO sat away from them.

IDA: Fucking Yanks! Where are they? I'll betcha they swagger up when it's nearly over, pick up all the dead men's hats, and make an 'ollywood film about how John Wayne won the fucking war on his whatsaname.

RENNIE: Horse?

IDA: Na!

LAURIE: Tod.

Enter HARVEY KLEINMAN in the uniform of a volunteer ARP warden. He is IDA's husband.

HARVEY: Ida, get your blackouts sorted will yer.

IDA: You might be my husband Harvey Kleinman, but I'm at work, you don't fucking tell me what to do, not in here, alright!

LAURIE: Ida, get your blackouts sorted will yer.

IDA complies. RENNIE laughs.

RENNIE: See Solomon's shop took a hit Harvey!?

HARVEY: Yeah, they're all dead, yeah, tragic.

HARVEY joins BENNY and HUGO.

D'yer get anyfin outa Solomon's place?

BENNY: Cutlery. Silver boxed sets. Hugo flogged 'em up West.

HUGO: Here you go Mr Kleinman…

HUGO empties his pockets of a bundle of notes. HARVEY takes the money and pockets it.

HARVEY: Now gimme the rest of the money, or that's the last you'll see of my daughter.

HUGO produces a five pound note, which HARVEY takes. In MASTER ATTAR's house. Night time. ATTAR is a middle-aged Bangladeshi, dressed like Noël Coward. ATTAR is writing in a big ledger.

MUSHI: Why do you want all the lascar names Sahib Master Attar?

ATTAR: Merchant navy captains do not know the names of our people. It's only port serangs in Calcutta, and me, know the names. Serangs are all bastards, so when a ship is torpedoed the Indian Embassy talk to me. I am the only man who can tell a father whether his son is alive or dead.

MUSHI: Abdul Quereshi, coala wallah; Ashraf Miah, agwallah; that's it. Except, young boy, Taz, don't know family name, sorry, sahib.

ATTAR: Don't call me sahib, I'm a socialist. SS Clan Macarthur. Thirty one lascars, and little Taz. (*He closes the book.*) Is your room to your liking?

MUSHI: Oh yes. Very nice. But you said I had to share the bed?

ATTAR: Don't worry, he's not English. Hasmat Miah, he works nights boiler room Savoy Hotel. I think you have attractive personality. I want you to run my chocolate raffle. Easy money for the right man.

MUSHI: Easier than renting beds?

ATTAR: That's it! Personality! The English love a joke! You buy a chocolate bar from me for a ha'penny –

MUSHI: – buy from you, the socialist!?

ATTAR: That's enough personality. Sell seven tickets at a penny each. Easy money. But first you must think of a new name. Clan Line give ten pounds for information about lascars who have swum the dock.

MUSHI: I come England one reason. Father say must find half Christian, half Jewish girl, make twins. This decreed by Allah. Boy twin I give mosque, he will bring whole world to God. Keep girl, but boy haram to me.

ATTAR: Bollocks! Your father had too many sons and no land to give you. He made up that shit so you would leave home feeling good.

MUSHI: My father would not lie! He is Pir, holy man, direct descendant Shah Jalal, he said girl have Jewish name. Seven letters, first letter D.

In the pub, it's evening and a piano player tinkles away. DEBORAH is still in overalls.

IDA: Oi Deborah!? You gonna give us a song tonight doll?!

DEBORAH: Giss a break Mum, I just done an eight hour shift ain't I!

Enter a small group of Indian LASCARS. Silence. IDA comes over.

IDA: Fucking...heroes! The Indian Lascars! The engine room of the British Merchant Navy! Standing shoulder to shoulder wiv us in the fight against whatsaname –

LAURIE: – Totalitarianism.

The pub stand and applaud the LASCARS. IDA leads the cheers. The LASCARS stand and bow.

IDA: For you boys, drinks are on the house!

SHAH ABDUL: Two teas please Miss.

EGG NOG: They're very religious miss. I'm not, I'll have a large Egg nog please no ice.

IDA: That's more like it son, you might fucking die tomorrow!

HARVEY, IDA, DEBORAH, BENNY and HUGO form a family group.

RENNIE: Amaaazin' woman, Ida, she's like Britannia herself boy!

LAURIE: Ida? She ain't English, she's Irish. Irish who married a Jew.

RENNIE: No! Harvey is never Jewish boy!

LAURIE: Harvey Kleinman not Jewish! He's as Jewish as 'the hole in the sheet'. That's the worst mix – Irish and Jewish. You end up with a family of pissed up burglars run by a clever accountant.

Enter MUSHI, with pinstripe suit, carnation, a trilby, and a pocket full of chocolate bars.

MUSHI: Chocolate raffle! Penny ticket, everyone got penny!

SOLDIER: One for me, one for the lady!

MUSHI: (*To the LADY, kissing her hand.*) Ahh, lovely eyes!

LADY: You're a fast worker ain't yer!

MUSHI: No time to waste! Hitler coming! Chocolate raffle! Penny ticket!

LAURIE: I'm the guvnor here. What's your name son?

MUSHI: Er… Mush.

LAURIE: Mister Mush, meet my barmaid, Ida, to you she's the Queen of England. You wanna work my pub mate, you give her a bar of chocolate first.

MUSHI: (*Gives chocolate.*) Queen Ida, salaam aleykum! A gift from East.

RENNIE: He's got some personality boy!

IDA: I like you Mister Mushi!

MUSHI moves over to EGG NOG and SHAH ABDUL.

MUSHI: Salaam aleykum!

EGG NOG / ABDUL: Aleykum salaam!

MUSHI: My post office Sandwip.

SHAH ABDUL: Unagon.

EGG NOG: Mirganjbazar –

MUSHI: – near Badeshwar?!

EGG NOG: Yes!

MUSHI: All Sylheti Brothers! Chocolate raffle! Penny ticket!

He approaches DEBORAH at the piano. LOVERS MUSICAL STING. She buys a ticket.

Lovely eyes.

DEBORAH: I bet you say that to all the girls.

MUSHI: Yes I do. But with you I am not lying.

DEBORAH: Number thirteen?!

MUSHI: Thirteen lucky with Mister Mushi.

HUGO: This better be proper chocolate – alright!

MUSHI: All man working clothes. What you do?

RENNIE: Go on Debs! Tell him what you do!

Chord on the piano. The Gracie Fields song. The whole pub joins in on the chorus.

Song: Thingummybob

The song ends.

IDA: It is an'all!

MUSHI: Queen Ida! Please! Make draw!

He offers the hat with all the tickets in to IDA to draw. Comic chord on the piano.

IDA: The winning ticket is…number thirteen!

DEBORAH: (*Screams.*) It's me!

She kisses MUSHI and takes the chocolate. MUSHI grabs her arm.

HUGO: Get your fucking black paws off her alright!

Chilled silence. HUGO approaches MUSHI and nuts him. MUSHI falls to the ground bleeding. An air raid siren. The pub empties, not in a panic, but with urgency. DEBORAH and MUSHI leave together.

DEBORAH: Air raid. Tube'll be rotten crowded. I know where we can be alone.

MUSHI: Oh fuck! Sorry I only got Merchant Navy English. Shit, bastard, fuck.

DEBORAH: I like you, Mister Mushi, you got personality.

MUSHI: How you spell Deborah?

DEBORAH: D. E. B. O. R. A. H.

MUSHI: Seven letters beginning with D.

DEBORAH: This is my Nan's shelter. She don't use it.

She links arms and pulls him into the Anderson shelter. The drone of the Luftwaffe begins

I love your skin. You're beautiful.

She kisses him, properly.

MUSHI: Are you maiden?

DEBORAH: Cheeky. Mind your own business. What about you?

MUSHI: Many commercial ladies. Every port – jiggy jiggy!

DEBORAH: Know what you doing then, eh? I like the war. Got me own money, wear what I like, do what I like. I don't want babies, well I wouldn't mind a girl. Be frightened Mushi. You gotta feel it.

MUSHI: I'm scared.

DEBORAH: They bomb the docks, and the docks are a little spit away. Hold me.

MUSHI holds her. A kiss.

The trick is to do something to stop thinking about the bombs.

She kisses him. A bomb falls, not that far off.

MUSHI: Agh!

DEBORAH: It missed us Mushi. It killed someone else.

MUSHI: Oh no, no, no!!

DEBORAH: Don't think about them, think about this.

She puts his hand on a breast.

Is that nice? Ha! I know that's nice, I can feel you.

MUSHI: Oh fuck!

DEBORAH: You're funny. Lie down.

MUSHI lies down. She slips the rest of her overalls off and gets in beside him. They make love during the bombing. Morning. MUSHI and DEBORAH asleep in each other's arms. On the street, ARPs and FIREMEN bring the dead out from Bethnal Green tube.

MILKMAN: Morning! Bomb hit the tube then?

FIREMAN 1: Na. Panic stampede. Hundred and seventy dead.

MILKMAN: Would you Adam and Eve it eh!? That's Harvey Kleinman. I'll tell his missus shall I?

FIREMAN 2: Someone has to.

MILKMAN: Yeah, but it's not usually the fucking milkman is it! Ha, ha!

MILKMAN goes off with a chuckle and a whistle and knocks on the Kleinmans' door. At this point HUGO and BENNY enter carrying a stolen wireless each.

Oh yeah, the early bird catches the worm.

HUGO: You wanna watch it mate, awight?!

MILKMAN: Fuck off you little dick. Benny, get your muvver out here. I need a word.

IDA opens the door. BENNY and HUGO go in.

(*Handing over the milk.*) Morning Ida. Pint of steri, pint of gold top.

IDA: Ta. What?

MILKMAN: Er… I've got some bad… I've got access to a bit of Cheddar.

IDA: Alright.

Cheddar handed over.

What is it Ted?

MILKMAN: There's been a panic stampede. Down the tube.

IDA: Oh no. Harvey. My Harvey! Is he alright?

MILKMAN: No. He's brown bread.

IDA goes off to the tube, wailing. Leaving MILKMAN on his own.

That went quite well I think.

MILKMAN moves off with a whistle. IDA stands over HARVEY's body.

IDA: I fucking loved him! I give him the whole of my life! DEBORAH!!!

DEBORAH wakes up. IDA sets off to the Anderson shelter. IDA opens the door without knocking. MUSHI sleeps on.

(*Breaking up.*) I don't think I can go on without him.

DEBORAH: Dad? Oh no. You got Benny. You got me.

IDA: Yeah. Who the fuck is that?

DEBORAH: Mister Mushi.

IDA: The chocolate raffle fellah?

DEBORAH: Yeah.

IDA: We'll be alright for chocolate then. Is he gentle wiv yer?

DEBORAH: I'm not gonna talk about it mum.

IDA: (*Breaking up.*) Your dad made love to me like a fucking film star!

DEBORAH: Put the kettle on. I'll be there in a tick.

LAURIE and RENNIE by an open grave.

LAURIE: I respected Harvey. You knew where you were with Harvey Kleinman.

RENNIE: He was a thief boy!

BENNY, HUGO, enter carrying the coffin. IDA and others follow. They start to lower the coffin.

LAURIE: He was an old fashioned East End thief. He'd break into your house, rob you blind, but he cared. That's the kind of inexplicable juxtaposition that makes the East End totally incomprehensible to outsiders.

IDA: I was gonna read a poem, out loud, but I've changed me mind. Instead I'm gonna say a word about Adolf Hitler – (*Breaking up.*) the man who has taken the love of my life from me! That word is 'CUNT!'

ALL: (*Murmurs of approval / and 'yeah cunt's / 'Hitler, what a cunt' etc.*)

IDA: Do you know what your dad would want most now girl?

DEBORAH: For me to marry Hugo.

IDA: And have a little baby girl. We could call her Harvey, after your dad.

DEBORAH: I was fourteen when I got engaged mom. Hugo was my first kiss.

IDA: This war's ruined you, who do you think you are?

DEBORAH: I'm the girl that makes the thing that drills the hole that holds the spring that drives the rod that turns the knob that works the thingummybob, mum.

IDA: Marry Hugo, then we can trust him. It's important in our line of work. You ain't a suffragette no more, so stop behaving like one, or you might get knocked down by an 'orse. You spent last night with a wog! What's all that about?

DEBORAH: I was alive in the morning. That's what that was about.

Enter MUSHI.

MUSHI: Deborah?!

BENNY: Not now mate! Alright!?

MUSHI looks at DEBORAH, she turns away. HUGO and BENNY follow MUSHI outside.

HUGO: Oi! Chocolate! I'm her fiancé.

MUSHI: English not good.

BENNY: That's not English mate, that's French.

HUGO: I'm gonna marry her.

MUSHI: No, no, no! You don't understand. She's mine. God, four centuries ago

BENNY grabs him by the throat.

BENNY: – Shut it! You fucking curried monkey.

Enter ATTAR with SHAH ABDUL, and EGG NOG. ATTAR is carrying the book.

ATTAR: Please accept my commiserations on the death of your father.

BENNY: You knew him?

ATTAR: I was burgled once, I presume it was him.

BENNY lets go of MUSHI. BENNY and HUGO back off.

BENNY: The wedding's tomorrow. You're not invited.

HUGO: One on one, you're fucking nothing!

HUGO and BENNY leave.

MUSHI: Master Attar. I can't live without her.

ATTAR: You'll die then. But you still have to work. Egg Nog needs a rice cook for his stupid cafe.

MUSHI: But I only cook rice on deck of ship.

EGG NOG: Easy menu, dal, rice, tikka chicken.

ATTAR: Egg Nog has set up a halal butchery.

MUSHI: Where?

EGG NOG: In my bathroom.

They enter the curry house.

See, tables, chairs, very nice.

ATTAR: And totally empty.

EGG NOG: All Indian lascars will come. Then the English.

ATTAR: Englishmen will never eat curry, they don't have the arse for it.

Bell as customers enter. EGG NOG leaves. ATTAR gets out the letters.

MUSHI: Why have you got the ship book?

ATTAR: In a minute. First your letters. Your father says 'Thank you for the money. Send some more, quick. Your uncle

wants you to marry his daughter, your cousin. Anjum.'
Photograph. Ugh! Very dark.

ATTAR gives MUSHI the letter and the photo. Enter EGG NOG.

EGG NOG: An Englishman with his wife! He want chicken!

ATTAR: Not chicken tikka! It's too dry! Drown the whole thing
in gravy.

EGG NOG: No! Just put some rice on there Mushi.

ATTAR: Ah, don't listen to me, only been in England thirty
years!

MUSHI: I can't marry my cousin. I must make twins with
Deborah and the boy twin will bring the whole world to
God.

ATTAR: Mushi, I ran away to sea because they beat me until I
learned the Koran.

MUSHI: You are hafiz?!

ATTAR: I can recite the Koran in Arabic, a language I do not
speak. One day I read it in Bengali. Next day, I read the
Bible, Old Testament. The day after that, the Bible, New
Testament. By the end of the week I was knackered. None
of those books mention dinosaurs. The Koran is the word
of God and he forgot to mention dinosaurs!

MUSHI: No God for you then?

ATTAR: I'm a trade unionist, a socialist, and an atheist. That's
the full box set.

MUSHI: You will go hell Master Attar. For me, paradise.

ATTAR: This is the only paradise you will ever know!

MUSHI: What? Bethnal Green?

ATTAR: Shattering isn't it?!

EGG NOG exits with the plate.

Mushi, my friend, I am going back home.

MUSHI: No! We need you here!?

ATTAR: The war at sea is over, so for Sylhet, that's the end of the killing. Six thousand lascars dead and I am the only man who knows their names. The book. I didn't know how to tell you, but SS Clan MacArthur –

MUSHI: – no, no, no!

ATTAR: Torpedoed east of Madagascar. Two weeks after you jumped ship.

MUSHI: Little Taz?!

ATTAR: All lascars dead. For Taz, I was thinking maybe, Tassaduq.

MUSHI: Yes, must be.

ATTAR: Our people need to know who died, and who lives. I will take the book from village to village. You will now be the top man in Bethnal Green.

MUSHI: Me?! Why not Egg Nog, why not Shah Abdul?

ATTAR: Personality.

MUSHI: Do I have to dress like Noël Coward?

ATTAR: No, that's a personal thing. Make Englishmen of these boys, that is the highest goal, and not easy, many English are not worthy of the title.

Enter EGG NOG carrying the chicken tikka, untouched.

EGG NOG: Too dry. He wants gravy. Masala up anything. Quick!

ATTAR: Tomato, spices, cream –

EGG NOG: Don't put cream in there! Tomato and cream, are you fucking mad!?

ATTAR: English like cream in everything!

EGG NOG: Stop it! Never seen such a bloody mess! What the hell do I call that!?

ATTAR: (*Laughing.*) Tikka disaster!

MUSHI: No. Chicken tikka masala.

ATTAR exits, with hugs leaving EGG NOG and MUSHI to carry on. In the street.

NEWS VENDOR: Hitler dead! Germany surrenders! West Ham fixtures!

A street party combined with wedding reception. Everyone.

IDA: We lost yer dad but we got fru!

Enter HUGO as groom, BENNY as best man. DEBORAH puts on a veil and takes HUGO's hand. Confetti. ATTAR and MUSHI watch as HUGO carries her across the threshold of IDA's house. A NEWSPAPER VENDOR comes on to the street. His cries and newspaper selling is accompanied by an animated history of the 1950s and 60s. On each line below the NEWS VENDOR sells one paper

NEWS VENDOR: Britain and France invade Suez!

Beatlemania sweeps Britain!

John Lennon marries!

Beatles bigger than Jesus!

West Ham win World Cup!

Paul marries!

John marries Yoko!

Beatles split!

1970 something. EGG NOG's curry house transforms into MUSHI's curry house defined by the grotesque mural style depictions of paradise, and a photo of the West Ham team. DEBORAH walks in wearing a skirt above the knee.

MUSHI: Deborah! I can see your knickers! In my country you would be stoned!

DEBORAH: I'm not in your country. You're in mine.

MUSHI: You have never eaten in my restaurant in thirty years.

DEBORAH: I thought this place was Egg Nog's.

MUSHI: Egg Nog is a gambler, the greyhounds. He'd put money on the hare if the odds were good. I paid off his debts in 1952. He gave me the lease. Nice, yes? How you say in English…subtle?

DEBORAH: Hugo won't come in here.

MUSHI: Does he know about us?

DEBORAH: Dunno. He's not stupid.

MUSHI: That was thirty years ago.

DEBORAH: The one thing he can do well is bear a grudge. I'm only here cos he's in the Scrubs. Unfortunately he's getting out next week.

She sits at a table. MUSHI gives her a menu. She looks at it.

MUSHI: Your legs, I remember, they go all the way up don't they?!

DEBORAH: Why ain't you married Mushi?

MUSHI: I am married. I just didn't want to tell you.

DEBORAH: Is she here?

MUSHI: I hope not. She's supposed to be in Chittagong. (*MUSHI shows a photo.*) That's her. Anjum. My cousin.

DEBORAH: Is that allowed in Bangladesh? Marrying your cousin.

MUSHI: Allowed?! It's nearly bloody compulsory. Three daughters. Rayhana, Anika, and little Labiba. I watch you. You don't have children.

DEBORAH: It ain't a proper marriage. I'm not home every night. I'm gonna go down the housing, get me own place. I woulda liked a little girl.

MUSHI: Life is not for fun! Not for women anyway! You've left it too late!

DEBORAH starts crying, and stands to leave.

DEBORAH: Yeah, alright, don't rub it in. I think I'd better go.

MUSHI: That night in the blitz is the single most beautiful thing that has ever happened to me.

He grabs her arm.

Sorry. Goodbye.

DEBORAH: You got hold of my arm Mushi.

He lets her go. She leaves. Enter SHAH ABDUL, and EGG NOG.

EGG NOG: Mushi, we need your advice. How do we bring wife over?

SHAH ABDUL: I don't like English Betty. All powder and paint. Must marry Muslim.

MUSHI: What will Indian country girl do here? Sit indoors all day, crying! You boys work hard, send money home, when you fifty, fuck off back Chittagong, marry Miss World, stay in bed all day like Georgie Best! Women and children will never come! Only if three things happen. One – big flooding in Sylhet –

NEWS VENDOR: – Cyclone devastates Northern India! No local people involved.

MUSHI: Two – Pakistan civil war.

NEWS VENDOR: Pakistan troops invade Bengal!

SHAH ABDUL: What three?

MUSHI: (*Looking over shoulder at NEWS VENDOR.*) Three – er… I dunno, British government threaten to bang door shut on Indians for good.

NEWS VENDOR: New Immigration Act! Next year! Read the details!

MUSHI: Better get the women over double quick!

During the song – the women and children arrive. The women wear saris with an Indian and Hindu influence. The RABBI shakes hands with SHAH ABDUL and hands over the keys. The Islamic crescent replaces the Star of David.

Song: Babi He Write Me Come!

ANJUM: Babi he write me come!

WOMEN: Rajrani London, Rajrani London

ANJUM: Babi he write me come!

WOMEN: London maya! London maya!

ANJUM: I tell him I got no English tongue

WOMEN: Cholit Basha Cholit Basha

ANJUM: Across the seven seas and thirteen rivers
              There is a paradise.

              Many people love me in Sylhet
              Everything you want is very cheap
              My father died in my arms
              What you sow is what you reap
              God helped me, I got away
              Across the seven seas and thirteen rivers
              Goodbye to Shah Jalal, I'll swear on my
                Koran
              I'll never see my mother again

ANJUM: Babi he write me come

WOMEN: Rajrani London, Rajrani London

ANJUM: Babi he write me come!

WOMEN: London maya! London maya!

ANJUM: I tell him I got no English tongue

WOMEN: Cholit Basha Cholit Basha

ANJUM: Across the seven seas and thirteen rivers
                 there is a paradise

The housing office. MUSHI is there with ANJUM, and his three daughters. MUSHI is wearing a West Ham scarf. They are talking to BARRY, the housing officer. Populating the waiting room are EGG NOG, SHAH ABDUL with wives. Enter IDA and DEBORAH. They take a ticket.

BARRY: Right there's your keys!

MUSHI: Three bed Rothschild Buildings!

BARRY: Deborah Gaskin!

IDA: (*Standing.*) Right girl! Leave the swearing to me!

IDA sits before BARRY, DEBORAH stands behind.

BARRY: I have your age down here as –

IDA: – Don't you get arsey wiv me sunshine!

DEBORAH: – Mum?!

BARRY: Are you what the sociology books call an East End matriarch?

IDA: No! I'm her fucking muvver!

BARRY: You muvvers don't run the East End any more. This is the Welfare State, and this interview is with 'the individual applicant' Deborah Gaskin.

IDA: She's not a fucking individual, she's my daughter, English, and Befnal Green for generations!

BARRY: Mrs Deborah Gaskin. Are you homeless at the moment?

IDA: Course she ain't homeless, they're in with me ain't they!

BARRY: (*Writing.*) Not homeless. No points. Children?

DEBORAH: No, I ain't.

IDA: Her father, the only man I ever loved, died fighting Hitler. Ain't that worth a point? How are these fucking Pakis getting their points?

BARRY: Can I ask you madam to moderate your language.

IDA: I apologise. How are these fucking Pakistanis getting their points?

She picks up a chair and, starts smashing it up.

Were they homeless in Pakistan? Course they weren't! I betcha if she had brown skin you'd give her an house just like that!

BARRY joins a National Front gathering, with HUGO and BENNY. HUGO sprays NF on the wall and PAKIS OUT. Others sell BRITISH BULLDOG.

SPEAKER: So, it's official GLC policy to exclude whites from Brick Lane?

BARRY: Offer Bengalis housing anywhere else, they won't take it, don't feel safe.

HUGO: They want a Paki ghetto!

An orator, the SPEAKER, takes the stand. DEBORAH, IDA, and MUSHI are there.

SPEAKER: The tragedy of my lifetime has been to see this great nation contaminated by inferior cultures, but who has the guts to talk about the problem?! Only the National Front dare speak the truth. BRITAIN IS FULL!

Cheering. Particularly HUGO, and BENNY.

IDA: My girl can't get an house!

SPEAKER: It is GLC policy to exclude whites from public housing in Brick Lane.

BENNY: They just throw their rubbish out the windows!

MUSHI: They are Indian country girls, they never heard of rubbish collection.

SPEAKER: The National Front has a policy to end this self-inflicted decline through repatriation of coloured immigrants with financial compensation!

MUSHI: Good morning, I been here thirty years. I fought Hitler! This is my current wife, full British passport. I invented Chicken Tikka Masala, now British staple diet! How much cash for me to bugger off!?

DEBORAH: He don't mean you Mushi!

HUGO: He fucking does!

SPEAKER: We will never allow this corner of England to become a Pakistani ghetto!

MUSHI: 'Bangladeshi' ghetto. We won independence in nineteen seventy-one!

HUGO: Do you want some!

SPEAKER: March with me! Assert the right of the Englishman to the housing he built –

MUSHI: My house, Rothschild Buildings, was built by Jews!

SPEAKER: – to the schools and hospitals our taxes pay for!

They march off. In the pub. At the bar, IDA, RENNIE, LAURIE. At a table, DEBORAH.

IDA: Fucking Pakis!

DEBORAH: Mum!?

IDA: They come here, but they don't wanna be English!

LAURIE: And what is it that defines the English Ida?

IDA: I believe in certain fings.

RENNIE: Yes, like what?!

IDA: Tolerance!

DEBORAH: You been slagging them all day!

IDA: O' course I slag 'em, that's free speech innit!

RENNIE: Integration boy! Integration!

LAURIE: How's a Muslim woman gonna integrate round here?

IDA: Get your arse tattooed, a crack habit and seven kids by seven dads!

They laugh. Enter MUSHI with West Ham scarf. It goes quiet.

MUSHI: Pint of mad dog please Ida. Quiet! What's the matter?

RENNIE: Gonna West Ham Mushi?

MUSHI: No! They're playing The Arsenal. I refuse to spend ten quid to watch an offside trap.

MUSHI joins DEBORAH at the table.

Did you get a house?

DEBORAH: You're joking ain't yer.

MUSHI: Please don't vote National Front. Not you.

DEBORAH: I can't hate you Mushi, you're lovely.

MUSHI: I have a flat, over the restaurant. It has a bathroom. Come.

They exit to the street, hiding from HUGO and BENNY who are talking to JANICE standing outside her terraced house with a FOR SALE/SOLD.

BENNY: What's occurring Janice?

JANICE: Bought me house off the council yesterday, sold it today, thirty grand profit. Gonna go Redbridge.

HUGO: Redbridge is shit!

JANICE: Yeah, I know. But it ain't Pakistan. Knowhatimean.

HUGO: I'm gonna kill myself a Paki tonight!

BENNY: One on one, they're fucking nothing!

MUSHI and DEBORAH are in the flat. It is a beautiful bedroom, with drapes, textiles, cushions. In the middle is the single bed from the Anderson shelter. Evening to night.

DEBORAH: That's my Nan's bed, from the shelter.

MUSHI: Yes. Our bed. That junk shop on Roman Road.

DEBORAH: Are you alright Mushi, or are you a bit weird?

MUSHI: I love you. That's all.

DEBORAH: I had a boyfriend couple of years ago, he had a mouth like yours. When I was with him I used to shut my eyes, and imagine he was you.

MUSHI: Kissing is very dangerous.

DEBORAH: Let's burn the house down.

They kiss. Dark falls. They spend the night together. On the street, BENNY and HUGO wait near the mosque. EGG NOG comes out, alone. They follow him, and walk either side of him.

HUGO: Poppadom, poppadom, poppadom…

BENNY: Got the right time, mate? I don't want Paki time. Ha!

EGG NOG: No watch, sorry boss.

HUGO: Just tell him the fucking time, you curried piece of shit!

EGG NOG: Going home, Bethnal Green Road.

They grab him. EGG NOG tries to remove HUGO's restraining hand.

BENNY: Don't you dare call Bethnal Green 'home'.

They both kick as EGG NOG offers no resistance. HUGO stabs him, killing him.

HUGO: See, I told yer, one on one they're fucking nothing!

BENNY: Chuck the knife.

HUGO chucks the knife off into the wings.

And get rid of that shirt.

HUGO: He's ruined it! I only nicked it yesterday. Your mum'll wash it for us.

HUGO and BENNY move off quickly. The sun comes up on the body of EGG NOG. CAMILLA opens her door to go to work. Sirens. ST JOHN follows her out into the street.

CAMILLA: What I love about Spitalfields, is the eclectic mix, all humanity is here.

ST JOHN: And the houses are cheaper than Hampstead.

CAMILLA: Hampstead? Yuk! All that sterile homogeneity! We're in the East End now St John, to live, to work, to make a difference.

ST JOHN: I think I've made a terrible mistake. I've married Sidney Poitier!

Sirens, a POLICEMAN attends the body. Bangladeshis gather round the corpse.

CAMILLA: A murder! Right on our doorstep. Oh, it's so visceral!

ST JOHN: Someone's been killed, and you sound pleased?

CAMILLA: I did my VSO in Cambodia. I need this edge or else I can't function.

She walks off to work.

ST JOHN: (*Shouted after her.*) You work in a library!

A couple of doors further along the street HUGO leaves, with a surreptitious glance to the dead body. IDA steps out after him.

IDA: Oi! What's with this washing then?

HUGO: Yeah. Industrial accident. Is that alright? Mum?

IDA: Yeah. Go on. Off you go.

In the mosque, the Bangladeshi men. Essentially in two factions, the older lascar types and the first generation, more militant, armed with sticks.

SHAH ABDUL: Let us not forget the teachings of Shah Jalal, must love fellow man.

NAZ: We gotta get ourselves some defence force.

SHAH ABDUL: My son, how dare you interrupt your father!

NAZ: Yeah, you're my father, and I respect you and all that, but if the police ain't gonna do nofing, we gotta do it for ourselves innit! Revenge!

SHAH ABDUL: Man kills man, son kill son, cousin kill cousin?! No! Everyone, go home, knock on neighbor door, say Salaam Aleykum. Peace be with you.

NAZ: I ain't gonna be knocking on no doors! We gotta defend our territory, we gotta arm ourselves, gotta fight back!

SHAH ABDUL: Quiet please! Let our community leader speak!

MUSHI: My first night in this country. Policeman, like Dixon of Dock Green, helped me find Master Attar house. 'England people very nice!' I say. He say 'Son, there's good and bad in all'. Such wisdom. One skinhead kill one of us doesn't mean all England people bad! We must behave like Englishmen, march to Parliament –

NAZ: – like good little Pakis!?

MUSHI: – I came this country to work, not to fight in the streets!

NAZ: That might be true for you old men, yeah, but I was born here! These streets is ours yeah, them skinheads ain't even got no right to come here!

Uproar. The young walk out. The crowd disperses. SHAH ABDUL approaches MUSHI.

SHAH ABDUL: You direct descendant Shah Jalal! Your father, direct descendant Shah Jalal! Your job – make twins! Give boy to mosque, then we have leader with blood Shah Jalal! But what did you do with sacred legacy Shah Jalal?! You opened curry house called it Shah Jalal Tandoori!

MUSHI: Yes, I have failed, all time in England, only interested in money, drinking. I blame Master Attar. He sent me to Natural History museum, learn about dinosaurs. And I lost my faith.

SHAH ABDUL: That big dinosaur, diplodocus, it's plastic.

MUSHI: No!? Is it?! But why didn't Allah tell the prophet about dinosaurs?

SHAH ABDUL: Do you shout your mouth off about your cock ups!?

MUSHI: Of course, Allah not want to look silly.

SHAH ABDUL: Go hajj, make pilgrimage to Mecca, remind Allah that you still fear him.

MUSHI: I'm too young for hajj, and anyway I don't like camping.

SHAH ABDUL: You one man! Our community, many people, you must make sacrifices!

MUSHI: OK, OK, I will lay with Deborah, try and make those twins.

SHAH ABDUL: Inshallah.

The BRICK LANE MASSIVE come out of the martial arts club. They're variously armed.

Song: Brick Lane Boys

> Gonna go Chicksand cut through Spellman
> hang out Hanif bottom of Redman

> Burn down Diss Street tear through Clare
>   Street
> Black mocassins like wheels on my feet
> Gonna go Brick Lane
> Gonna go insane
> Sex and pills let loose in my brain
> Brick Lane BoyZ Brick Lane BoyZ
> Curtains hairstyles, cars like toys
> Brick Lane BoyZ Brick Lane BoyZ
> Get together and make some noise
> Faz is a pill boy, Raz is a crack head
> Nizam's gotta get a girl into bed
> All street fighters, and brown rap writers
> Red box igniters and rude girl delighters
> Gonna go Brick Lane
> Gonna go insane
> Sex and pills let loose in my brain

During the next a lone skinhead, is knocked down, then hands over a street sign. Then he gets up, is knocked down again and hands over another street, knocked down again etc.

> Warden, Nelson, Sugar Loaf, Wellington
> Fournier, Rhoda, Old Nichol Street
> Brady, Buxton, Russia, Hoxton,
> Hopetown, Hanbury, Jamaica Street
> Brick Lane BoyZ Brick Lane BoyZ
> Curtains hairstyles, cars like toys
> Brick Lane BoyZ Brick Lane BoyZ
> Get together and make some noise

ST JOHN enters. He has a laptop in a case on a shoulder strap. They surround him.

NAZ: What have you got for me today man?

ST JOHN: You don't want to mug me. I live round here.

NAZ: We ain't gonna jack you man? Don't wanna disrespek ya. We just want de laptop, and yo cash yeah? And dat nice watch innit. Alright. Easy?!

ST JOHN suddenly spins away and twirls his lap top round with the shoulder strap. They laugh.

ST JOHN: Come and get it! I'm army trained! Who wants to die first!?

One of them takes his legs from under him and then they kick him badly. They take his laptop. MUSHI comes on the scene.

MUSHI: Get off him! Naz, I know your father, religious man, and look at you!

NAZ: Go chew khat old man.

MUSHI: (*Helping ST JOHN.*) Here, can you stand? I apologise on behalf of Bangladesh. Our young boys don't respect their elders.

ST JOHN: That's something they've learned from us.

MUSHI: Ah! So you're a liberal!

ST JOHN: How can you tell?

MUSHI: Only a liberal blames himself when he gets mugged.

They shake hands and MUSHI leaves. In the flat. DEBORAH is there, enter ANJUM.

DEBORAH: Oh my God!

ANJUM: Don't scare! I am his current wife.

DEBORAH: Anjum? Nice to meet you.

ANJUM: He's a good lover isn't he? Very quick. He give me three lovely girls.

ANJUM shows her a framed photograph.

Labiba, good English, all poetry; Rayhana, she like children. Anika, she want go University, but very lucky, I find her husband. I don't mind you / him just afternoons. No-one know, OK?

Enter MUSHI.

Thumy dong dheksony, armi thumur fiet safkormu.
Bashtar Kowari!

ANJUM leaves. During the next MUSHI starts to undress in preparation for love making.

DEBORAH: What did she say?

MUSHI: She's not that keen on cleaning this flat. Now! I have to make love to you, properly, not to pass the time but to make twins! The boy I give to the mosque, the girl you can keep.

DEBORAH: I'm married to Hugo.

MUSHI: Come on! I've got the whole community on my back!

DEBORAH: There'll be a girl? I can keep the girl?

MUSHI: Yes! I've got bloody three already. Get your kit off!

DEBORAH: If I get pregnant, there's gonna be a bump. Hugo –

MUSHI: – You divorce Hugo, marry me.

DEBORAH: What about your wife, Anjum?

MUSHI: What's it got to do with her?!

DEBORAH: Come on then sailor, make love to me.

They kiss. Pockets of people are watching TV. There is a collective gasp as the first plane hits the towers.

What was that?

MUSHI: It sounded like the whole world screaming.

DEBORAH: I love these moments, when there's only me and you.

The second plane hits the towers. A second collective gasp.

What the bloody hell is that?!

MUSHI: Something really very terrible is happening. Wait here!

MUSHI runs out into the street.

SHAH ABDUL: Mushi! Terrorists fly airliner into twin towers.

MUSHI: What?! Wembley!?

SHAH ABDUL: New York, World Trade Centre.

MUSHI: No! This is all my fault! Lord, forgive me, I am trying now, I am trying.

In the pub. The usual suspects.

LAURIE: Says here, terrorists go to paradise where there's seventy-two sex slaves each, as much booze as you can drink, and lots of beautiful fountains.

RENNIE: I bet there's a fuck of a queue for the fountains boy!

Enter BARRY.

LAURIE: Alright Barry!?

IDA: You're that bloke from the housing! I ain't serving you!

BARRY: I told you Mrs Kleinman, the only way you're gonna get a council house if you're white is tell your doctor you're suicidal – pills is points.

IDA: I went to my doctor, told him I was suicidal, he wunt give me no pills, he offered me fucking counselling!

LAURIE: What you doing in my manor then Barry?

BARRY: Giving houses away to refugees. This one's got three wives.

IDA: It's illegal innit, whatsaname.

LAURIE: Polygamy.

BARRY: He gets full social for the first wife, thirty quid each for the other two. That's how fucking illegal it is.

IDA: Laurie, I'm off down York Hall for me whatsaname.

LAURIE: Women-only naked steam.

IDA leaves.

RENNIE: Women-only naked steam eh?! Be like Muslim heaven boy!

LAURIE: Seventy-two?! That's an unnecessary amount of sex slaves innit. I'd be happy enough with thirty or forty.

BARRY: You not getting enough Laurie?!

LAURIE: The last time I had sex, not only was Gary Glitter a free man, he was in the charts.

In the street. NAZ and RAYHANA are whitewashing over a Spearmint Rhino poster. LABIBA is handing out Sharia law leaflets. Passers by take leaflets. LABIBA is in hijab, RAYHANA in niqab.

LABIBA: Take a leaflet bruvver, and you muvver, read and discover. We're celebrating the Shaheed today, the ones wot blew you away, Mohammad Attar, who is now a martyr, and the glorious 19, the mujahideen, living clean in the Deen. Yeah.

Enter IDA she addresses the next line to the painters.

IDA: Oi! You can't do that!

NAZ: Go home, get dressed, whore!

IDA: What you call me yer little twat?!

LABIBA: He call ya a whore lady. Yeah.

NAZ: You're gonna have to dress modest round here now! Showing your everything, what are you grandma, sixty, seventy!

IDA: I could fucking eat you and spit you out! Hang on, I know your father! Oi Mushi, you seen this!?

MUSHI: Naz, ah, good you got a job at last eh?

IDA: Yeah, you're Shah Abdul's lad. You're the drug dealer.

NAZ: I don't mess with that shit no more.

LABIBA: He fought his personal jihad against drugs, yeah, come out glorious and victorious. Yeah.

RAYHANA: Don't get involved Dad.

MUSHI: Don't call me Dad! I'm old enough to be your father!

RAYHANA: You are my father.

MUSHI: Agh! Labiba! And Rayhana! Why you both gone hijabi?!

LABIBA: We celebrating, Sheik Osama, 9/11, and the mujahadeen in heaven.

MUSHI: Celebrating 9/11, in the street?! You've gone mad!?

LABIBA: The ummah is strong, this is our year, we got no fear.

MUSHI: Stop bloody rhyming will you!

RAYHANA: We're gonna clean up this manor with the Sharia Dad.

MUSHI: Where's Anika? Has she gone hijabi?

LABIBA: Anika is lost to her sisters. We gonna declare her Takfir.

MUSHI: Takfir! Don't talk about your sister like that. Go home! Stop this. Later, I'll give you both the maximum bollocking. Naz!? I'm going to see your father now!

MUSHI goes to the Mosque to find SHAH ABDUL, who is coughing.

I have bad news for you my friend. Your son is mentally ill. He's celebrating 9/11 in the middle of Whitechapel Market.

SHAH ABDUL: I want to beat him, but I am weak.

MUSHI: Your lungs are like mine, full of Merchant Navy coal.

SHAH ABDUL: (*Coughs.*) He is a wild man now.

MUSHI: Drugs?

SHAH ABDUL: No thanks, I'll have a lie down later.

MUSHI: My daughters gone hijabi, and they bully my wife into niqab! One minute I'm living with four beautiful Indian women, next minute I've got a house full of bloody Arabs!

SHAH ABDUL stands, picks up some library books.

SHAH ABDUL: Come with me.

MUSHI: Where are we going?

SHAH ABDUL: I have a meeting with the top lady in Tower Hamlets. Naz has been reading books from the council library.

MUSHI: I was looking for heroin one day under Labiba's bed, and I find all jihadi books from the library, and even worse –

SHAH ABDUL: – (*Stopping in his tracks.*) Terrorism manuals?

MUSHI: – no, the books were all overdue.

SHAH ABDUL: Our community lacking leadership. Is she pregnant yet?

MUSHI: Don't put the pressure on.

SHAH ABDUL: Maybe you're firing blanks.

MUSHI: No! I've been tested. I had to give a sample. They didn't give me a DVD, magazine, nothing.

SHAH ABDUL: What did you do?

MUSHI: I had to close my eyes and think of Shilpa Shetty.

CAMILLA's office in the town hall. She has access to a computer. Enter SHAH ABDUL and MUSHI.

CAMILLA: Salaam Aleykum

SHAH ABDUL: Hi.

CAMILLA: How can I help?

SHAH ABDUL: In Bethnal Green, we are from Sylhet, our Islam you could call it Sufi, our path to Allah is meditation, music, devotional poetry –

MUSHI: – we don't fly aeroplanes into buildings!

SHAH ABDUL: This your library book, my son renewed it seven times. *Milestones* –

MUSHI: – How many copies do you have? Ask the computer!

CAMILLA types in a search on the laptop.

SHAH ABDUL: Sayyid Qutb, author, hates the West. Hates! Everything!

CAMILLA: Tower Hamlets libraries have eleven copies of *Milestones.*

MUSHI: Eleven!? Bloody hell!

SHAH ABDUL: Mushi's daughters have books by –

MUSHI: – and tapes. Bilal Philips. How many copies you have!?

CAMILLA types in a search.

SHAH ABDUL: This man preaches all Wahhabi. This is all crazy Saudi Islam as political ideology. Nothing to do with Sylhet! He is Jamaican convert!

CAMILLA: Bilal Philips – eighty books and tapes.

MUSHI: (*Standing.*) Eighty! You are using my taxes to teach my children to hate their own country!

CAMILLA: I am committed to delivering equivalent services regardless of race, religion, gender, disability or sexual orientation. And, I didn't become a professional librarian to ban books.

SHAH ABDUL: Me, two years German prisoner of war camp. If you stock one copy *Mein Kampf,* that free speech, you stock eighty copies, you Nazi yourself!

Beat. Then an explosion, they all stand, there is a second, louder, explosion, followed by a third explosion, then a fourth. In the pub. LAURIE, BARRY, IDA and RENNIE is dancing with joy.

RENNIE: – Rivers of blood! Ha, ha, ha! Enoch Powell was right boy! He only got one thing wrong! It's not us boy! It's not us! Ha, ha!

LAURIE: I'm not BNP Barry, but these tube bombings gotta be good for you eh?

BARRY: We're absolutely fucking flying mate. Little things help. Today Tower Hamlets banned Christmas decorations in the offices. Health and Safety.

RENNIE: Health and Safety my arse!

IDA: My women-only naked steam, that's gone, gotta dress modest now. That's my culture that is, since way back, before the whatsanames –

LAURIE: – Romans.

RENNIE: How do you dress modest in a women-only naked steam?

LAURIE: I would consider voting BNP, if you had some black candidates.

BARRY: It won't be long before my party does have a black candidate. After 9/11, and today, skin colour is irrelevant. Culture. That's where the battle is. Take Rennie, he's black, but he's as British as hot tea in a flask.

RENNIE: We came here to work!

BARRY: But to Islamists he's a kaffur.

RENNIE: What's that boy?

BARRY: Kaffur. It means nigger. You're a nigger again Rennie, how's that make you feel? The good news is, I'm a kaffur an'all. We're brothers.

BARRY exits. RENNIE is distressed, contemplative. LAURIE moves over to comfort him.

LAURIE: If you take a little plastic Santa Claus, file his head down to a point, then poke yourself in the eye with it repeatedly. You could hurt yourself.

RENNIE doesn't laugh. He looks at LAURIE and stands, and leaves the pub, passing MUSHI and DEBORAH as they enter. DEBORAH is crying. They find a table, away from LAURIE/RENNIE

IDA: What's the matter doll?

MUSHI: Twins! We've had the scan down the London!

IDA: I'm gonna be a fucking grandmuvver!

DEBORAH: – Mum! This is not good news! I'm married to Hugo!

IDA: I can put Hugo in the Scrubs for good. He killed Egg Nog.

MUSHI: Hugo kill Egg Nog?!

IDA: He give me his shirt to wash. Covered in blood it was, brand new Ben Sherman. I never washed it. I didn't want to be a whatsaname –

LAURIE: – accessory to the crime.

IDA: I bought the exact same shirt, put it through the wash. I got the blood stained Ben Sherman in the freezer in the back room here.

MUSHI: Champion! Ida take the bag down to the police station. Hugo goes to prison for evermore, and we can all get married!

IDA: What? Deborah marry you and move in. What about your wife? What about your daughters?

MUSHI: My daughters? No worries! They're all good girls.

In MUSHI's. LABIBA and RAYHANA with a computer. RAYHANA is on the mouse. Enter ANIKA.

LABIBA: Just click download man!

RAYHANA: Snow White and the Seven Dwarfs?

LABIBA: Yeah, you teaching that shit at your nursery, yeah, and this scholar says it's a koof conspiracy, promoting promiscuity, in da Muslim community.

RAYHANA: Can't open it. It's a PDF file.

LABIBA: We ain't got Adobe Acrobat!? Where did dad pick up dis gay compu'er?

ANIKA: Comet.

LABIBA: Man! Comet is a washing machine shop.

ANIKA: OK sister, *you* explain how Snow White is an attack on Muslim marriage?

LABIBA: Innit obvious man?! You got one girl living wiv seven dwarves and there ain't one of them midgets big enough to marry her!

ANIKA: Dad bought us this computer to share, I've got Uni work I need to do.

RAYHANA: Facebook.

LABIBA: (*Laughing.*) Yeah, some kuffar poked you today innit. Gary!

RAYHANA: Gary wants to know can he come on your flashmob iftar if he ain't a Muslim.

ANIKA: How come you know my password?

RAYHANA / LABIBA: Sisters!

ANIKA: OK, I can see where you two been. Rule number one with this computer – don't dowload shit. There's three beheading videos filed in iTunes.

LABIBA: I can't watch them beheadings! I have to look at the floor man!

RAYHANA: You can't tell us wot to do when you're on Facebook all the time.

LABIBA: Grooming the kuffar!

RAYHANA: Have the mosque approved your 'flashmob iftar'?

ANIKA: We're giving charity, zakat, you remember zakat do you Rayhana?

RAYHANA: It ain't zakat what you're doing, giving food to alcoholics.

ANIKA: Zakat should be local. The hungry round here are in Museum Gardens.

LABIBA: Man! They're not 'the hungry', they're 'the pissed'.

RAYHANA: Them tramps in Museum Gardens ain't Muslims.

ANIKA: Where does it say that zakat is just for Muslims?

RAYHANA: Ain't that kinda obvious?

ANIKA: That might be your faith, but it ain't mine.

LABIBA: Don't talk about faith sister, you're takfir!

ANIKA: Hey, look who learned another Arab word today! If people see my flashmob iftar on telly, they might stop thinking that all British Muslims spend every evening sitting in the garage boiling down hair dye!

LABIBA: This is your public relations, you tryna make the nation, understand the situation, get less apprehensive, about the Muslim offensive.

ANIKA: Don't record your rhymes on this shared computer. We could end up in Paddington Green cos of that last rap or yours. Technically, it's criminal.

LABIBA: It ain't that bad, and it ain't a rap, it's resistance
rhyme.

RAYHANA: Is it a new one?

LABIBA: 'Improperganda'.

RAYHANA: That's clever. I wanna hear it.

LABIBA: Sister, it ain't never too late look
to quit your kuffar Facebook,
paradise waitin'
stop procrastinatin'
hate the disbelievers
they tryna deceive us
they will never believe us
Sheik Osama lead us
Shakespeare was a gay boy
knowhatisayboy
he get in the way boy
promoting fornication
to the Muslim nation
is not a situation
get my participation
it's improperganda
I don't misunderstand ya
I'm gonna get clean
halal living in the deen
God Save the Queen
I won't standfa that hymn
I follow Mohammad
Peace be upon him!

RAYHANA: Woo!

*ANIKA leaves the room with a slam of the door. In the pub. RENNIE
sitting silent, uncommunicative. LAURIE is reading the paper.
No IDA.*

LAURIE: Alright Rennie?

RENNIE stares at his pint, doesn't reply.

Talk to me. You're my best mate, you cunt.

RENNIE: This young boy, spit at me in the Post Office.

LAURIE: No!

RENNIE: In the queue. All these veiled women, you should see the money they picking up boy! They must have enough children! You work, you pays your stamp! Every week a stamp!

LAURIE: That is the central concept of insurance, you got to pay in, to get out.

RENNIE: Five year old, six year old. He looked me in the eye and spat at me.

LAURIE: Let me get you a drink Rennie. Cockspur? A little taste of Barbados. A glass of sunshine.

LAURIE gets a bottle of Cockspur rum from behind the counter and two glasses. He rejoins RENNIE and pours out two glasses.

RENNIE: Yeah.

LAURIE: Cheers. I can't wait to tell Ida. Ha, ha! That'll get her going.

RENNIE: Where is she?

LAURIE: Down the London. Deborah's started. They reckon it's twins.

RENNIE: Twins! Come on boy! We'd better have another drink!

They drink again. IDA arrives, unseen by LAURIE, seen by RENNIE.

What about you and Ida? Have you ever tried it on?

LAURIE: The boat race ain't too bad. And, you don't look at the mantlepiece when you're poking the fire but there's one big problem with Ida.

RENNIE: She got one helluva temper boy!?

LAURIE: All that 'fucking this and fucking that' – that's all an act Rennie, deep down she's just a little girl who early on lost the love of her life, Harvey Kleinman. They was neighbours, in the Rothschild buildings. Hers was Irish Catholics, his was Jewish. But one day they got Ida in to rake the coals on the Sabbath, they can't work on the Sabbath can they, yeah, she was what they call the Shabbes Goy. And that's how she first met Harvey. It was love at first sight. He was six, she was five. They married as soon as they could, on her fourteenth birthday. What is the greatest love story ever told? Romeo and Juliet? Elizabeth Bennet and Colin Firth. No. Harvey Kleinman and Ida Houlihan. Why? Cos theirs was an impossible love, a forbidden love. They didn't even know it was wrong.

RENNIE: They got competition now – Deborah and Mushi.

LAURIE: Debs is only following in her mother's footsteps. Ida was the pioneer. The first. The Sherpa Tenzing of cross cultural romance. All these different faiths, why do they wanna live separate? They're scared. They fear the power of love, because love laughs at the manufactured made up madness of religion and culture. What Ida did was monumental, so even though Harvey's dead, he still fills her up.

(*Cracks.*) There'll never be room for me mate. Sorry, I've upset meself.

RENNIE: (*Standing.*) I gotta go boy.

RENNIE leaves. LAURIE turns aware that IDA is there.

LAURIE: Oh fuck! How long you been –

IDA: – long enough.

IDA: I'm a fucking grandma Laurie!

LAURIE: Where they all gonna live?

IDA: There's a flat empty on Mushi's landing, so they've gone down the housing today.

LAURIE: Good luck to 'em.

IDA: Harvey don't fill me up no more. I've got room for you Laurie.

LAURIE: Yeah? Well…what if er… I mean there's nothing to stop us, you know, you and me, we could be together properly, you know, in whatsaname.

IDA: – Holy matrimony?!

LAURIE: Yeah!

In the Steiner nursery. RAYHANA, is wearing a niqab. Enter CAMILLA and ST JOHN.

CAMILLA: This is Galaxy's father, St John. Rayhana is Mister Mushi's daughter.

ST JOHN: Hi.

ST JOHN offers his hand to be shaken, RAYHANA refuses to shake it.

CAMILLA: We love the Steiner method.

ST JOHN: We also love the Montessori method, but you're cheaper.

RAYHANA: Galaxy is a lovely girl and –

CAMILLA: – I think she's potentially extraordinary.

RAYHANA: Her use of the sensorial equipment is normal. Her reading –

CAMILLA: – She's dyslexic, isn't she!? I told you!

RAYHANA: – is normal. However, in creative activity she fails to use her imagination but simply regurgitates stories from Walt Disney.

CAMILLA: (*Devastated.*) Oh my God! Really?!

RAYHANA: If you ask her to draw a monster, she'll draw Shrek.

ST JOHN: Shrek is Dreamworks, not Disney.

RAYHANA: Does she watch a lot of American DVDs at home?

CAMILLA: We try to limit –

ST JOHN: – yes, she does. We're both very busy, self-obsessed, and normally, in the evenings, a bit pissed.

CAMILLA: St John's been mugged. He's changed. He's started reading the *Spectator*.

RAYHANA: It's not normal for a British child to take all her culture from America.

ST JOHN: I refuse to be lectured to about 'normality' by a woman wearing a two-man tent.

CAMILLA: St John!?

ST JOHN: The girls in this nursery wear headscarves. Is it normal for a British five-year-old never to feel the sun on the back of her neck? You refused to shake my hand. Is that 'normal' behaviour for a grown up?

CAMILLA: She can't shake your hand, you know that!

RAYHANA: I'm sorry you were mugged. Those boys in those gangs are not Muslims.

ST JOHN: And yet, in the street, they shout 'whore' at Camilla.

CAMILLA: I think that's meant as a compliment.

ST JOHN: What makes someone Muslim?

RAYHANA: I can only give ten minutes to each set of parents.

MUSHI and DEBORAH with the pram in the waiting room of the housing department. BARRY is there behind his screen. A family of Somalis are at the counter.

DEBORAH: If you think I'm gonna give my baby boy to Shah Abdul, you must be nuts!

MUSHI: The boy is haram to me! I have to give him to the mosque and will bring the whole world to God! What's the problem, you get to keep the bloody girl! We go straight to the mosque after we get this flat sorted.

DEBORAH: I am not giving a baby to Shah Abdul, an old man, dying of emphysema.

MUSHI: He can get baby milk delivered from Tesco.com.

The Somali family are given keys and leave.

Look, Somalis. He gave them keys. They don't even speak English.

DEBORAH: They're refugees Mushi, there's a war on in Somalia.

MUSHI: Yes, and who started it? They did!

BARRY: Mister Rasul!

MUSHI and DEBORAH and pram go forward to the counter.

DEBORAH: Hello Barry.

BARRY: I don't know you Deborah. I'm at work. Understood.

MUSHI: We are seven now in a three-bed, sixteen Rothschild House, but the flat across the landing is now empty, they've gone Redbridge, if you give us that flat, we'll all be together.

BARRY: Like a village? Eighteen Rothschild House…has just been allocated.

MUSHI: Look Barry, Rothschild House is long time all Bangladeshi block. Works very well, no skinheads, good sense of community. Are you telling me you've given that flat to Somalis? Are they British! British passport!?

BARRY: Most people find that it helps if you smash up that chair.

MUSHI: This one?

BARRY: Yeah.

MUSHI picks up the chair and during the next smashes it against the glass. Enter NAZ

MUSHI: You can't give our houses away to Africans! I love this country! What gives you the right to ruin my bloody country!

DEBORAH: Mushi!

NAZ: It's me dad innit. He's fing.

MUSHI: Fing?

NAZ: Yeah.

MUSHI: Oh no. Deborah, we have to go to the mosque now.

DEBORAH: I told you I ain't going.

NAZ: Is this him then? The direct descendant of Shah Jalal?

MUSHI: Yes, that is the holy man.

NAZ: The new imam says he wants him to speak at the next Friday prayers.

MUSHI: When's that?

NAZ: Friday.

DEBORAH: He can't speak. He's only a day old.

NAZ: Jesus Christ spoke straight away, in the cradle, that's true lady, believe, that is what the Koran say.

DEBORAH: You can have whatever grand expectations you bloody like of my baby, sunshine and I hope he disappoints you! Me? I'm his mother and I'll be happy if he gets into Tech College. (*To MUSHI.*) I'll be in the pub.

She leaves with the pram.

MUSHI: (*To NAZ.*) Don't worry Naz. She'll come round. Let's go to the mosque now, see your father.

In the pub. DEBORAH is there with the twins in the pram. LAURIE is wearing a wedding button hole, and IDA is a bit dressed up, but not overly. IDA staring into the pram.

IDA: Ain't she beautiful. And look at him! Look at his little whatsaname –

LAURIE: – Penis.

IDA: Face!

DEBORAH: Where you been mom?

IDA: Been down the registry office. How mad am I? I fucking married him.

DEBORAH: Congratulations. Did you think of inviting your own daughter?

IDA: Didn't want to make a fuss.

DEBORAH: Who was your witness? Rennie?

IDA: Supposed to be but he didn't turn up.

LAURIE: I'm worried about him.

DEBORAH: Not like him not to be sat there. Laughing.

IDA: Come on Debs! What is it? You can tell me, I'm your muvver!

DEBORAH: Mushi wants to give the boy to the mosque.

IDA: Why's that then?

DEBORAH: He's gonna save the world, or something.

IDA: I can beat that for a problem.

DEBORAH: Don't tell me. Hugo.

IDA: Our Benny went to see him today, in prison. They're letting him out next week. Good behaviour.

DEBORAH: That is all we need. Does he know about me and Mushi?

IDA: Yeah. He says he's gonna kick the shit outa you, and throw you out the house. For me, for grassing him up, he's gonna rip my head off and shit down me neck.

DEBORAH: What we gonna do mum?

In SHAH ABDUL's house. The body is laid out on the bed. NAZ is there, as is ANIKA, and the blind IMAM ie: IQBAL with false beard on, hooks for hands etc. MUSHI touches the corpse.

MUSHI: You crossed the seven seas and thirteen rivers looking for paradise. You got it now and no mistaking. You deserve it my friend.

LABIBA: Where's the boy dad?

MUSHI: Labiba!? Why aren't you in bloody school?

LABIBA: I bunked off innit, cos I wanna hear this new imam speak.

NAZ: He's gonna speak now, like a study circle. They won't let him in Brick Lane mosque.

MUSHI: Of course they won't, they're not stupid.

NAZ: We're getting a new mosque.

LABIBA: We're told, it's gonna be gold, gonna be fixed, for the Olympics.

MUSHI: What is he? Saudi?

NAZ: Yeah, all their oil yeah, is for the ummah, the caliphate.

LABIBA: Inshallah, mashallah!

The IMAM starts speaking.

IMAM: You Muslims living in the West, you care more about how often your bins are emptied, than how your women dress. If a farmer wants to judge a bull, he does not look at the bull, he has a look at what the cows are up to. And Allah will judge you! In *Jew York,* (*Laughs.*) my little joke, in *Jew York* the women there had no discipline. (*Laughs.*) And then they were disciplined! (*Laughs.*) A woman must suck the snot from your nostrils if you ask her to!

MUSHI stands in disgust, and makes to leave.

NAZ: You gotta bring the boy Mushi, tonight. He's ours.

LABIBA: The boy to you is haram, understan', we is halal, and you is dajal!

MUSHI leaves.

IMAM: A woman is like a piece of pure white silk. One stain on the white silk and that silk is shit forevermore. (*Laughs.*) Ashahadu an la ilaha ill Allah wa ashahadu anna Muhammadar Rasullah.

The pub. IDA, LAURIE and DEBORAH with twins. They're still wearing button holes. Enter RENNIE. He has an overcoat on, and is carrying a suitcase.

IDA: Where you going love?

RENNIE: Home.

IDA: What d'yer mean home? Vallance Road's your home love.

RENNIE: Barbados.

LAURIE: No!?

RENNIE: Heathrow by two o'clock.

LAURIE: No liquids, no shaving foam, no jam. You can't take jam on a flight. How much jam have you got in there Rennie?

They look at the suitcase as if it might have a bomb in it.

RENNIE: Jam? I don't have no jam.

LAURIE: Terrorists, they've destroyed us, psychologically, since when have the English been terrified of marmalade?

IDA: You can't leave us Rennie. You got a good job. Fresh air, outdoors, nature.

RENNIE: I'm a postman.

DEBORAH: Bye Rennie.

RENNIE: Did you get a house?

DEBORAH: You're having a laugh ain'tcha. Wouldn't give us nothing.

RENNIE: Somalis?

DEBORAH: Yeah.

RENNIE: I got them living upstairs from me boy!

LAURIE: They're laughing at us.

DEBORAH hugs RENNIE.

IDA: Can we come wiv yer! We could claim whatsaname!

LAURIE: Political asylum.

RENNIE: Goodbye Ida.

RENNIE has gone.

LAURIE: I've known him years. I don't want no-one else to sit in that chair!

Enter MUSHI.

DEBORAH: Mushi, I've decided, I'm not letting you give my boy away!

MUSHI: Those wannabe-Arabs are not getting our boy and that's final!

DEBORAH: Why have you changed your mind love?

MUSHI: They've all gone Wahabi!

DEBORAH: You're out of the frying pan and into the fire cos Hugo's getting out next.

MUSHI: Oh no!

IDA: He'll kill me, kill you, kill Deborah, and kill the twins.

MUSHI: Alright, let me think!?

DEBORAH: What are we gonna do Mushi? Where can we go?

MUSHI: I got it! Yes! I know where we can go, and be safe, and happy.

DEBORAH: Where?

MUSHI: Redbridge!

SNAP TO BLACK.

Act Four (Epilogue)

PHILIPPA: Terrific! I'm not going to give any notes, from now on, you're on your own. I just want to say thank you, and good luck tonight.

YAYAH: Can I say something please! Thank you! Iqbal wants to say something.

IQBAL: Many of us were sceptical about a play showing how England *welcomed* immigrants, mainly because we are here imprisoned.

Some laughter.

TAHER: Take the beard off!

YAYAH: Shut up man, he's making his speech!

IQBAL takes the beard off.

IQBAL: I left Yemen to seek asylum in England. I am not here to turn England into Yemen. If England ever does become Yemen, I will have to seek refuge in another country. Philippa, we wanted to buy you a present but the most expensive thing in the shop is a Snickers bar. Here it is, not just a chocolate bar but a metaphor for much love, and gratitude.

He gives the Snickers bar to PHILIPPA who is nearly in tears.

PHILIPPA: Thank you. Thank you. Oh God, I'm overcome, really. Thank you.

She starts to cry. Enter OFFICER KELLY. He's still in costume but wearing his Officer hat.

OFFICER KELLY: Right. Got some envelopes here. Tatyana, Elmar, Taher, Iqbal, Yayah.

SANYA: Do you have an envelope for me?

OFFICER KELLY: Sorry. The bus is here, we're behind already. Come on! Chop, chop.

OFFICER KELLY goes off as do all the asylum seekers who don't have envelopes. YAYAH walks off whilst at the same time tearing his envelope up and reading the letter. TATYANA, ELMAR and TAHER sit and open their envelopes. PHILIPPA recovers and stands looking at those seated opening their envelopes. ELMAR stands to leave.

ELMAR: Thank you Philippa. You are a very talented director.

PHILIPPA: Elmar, if I can help, a friend of mine is a film producer –

ELMAR: – No. Not necessary.

He turns his back and leaves. TATYANA having read her letter stands, brushes past PHILIPPA and leaves quite energised.

TAHER: I apologise. I am sorry I am like I am. I have always been like this.

TAHER leaves.

OFFICER KELLY: Come on! Let's be having you!

Everyone leaves, except OFFICER KELLY, who from upstage watches IQBAL read his letter. IQBAL folds the letter and sits. KELLY realises what is going on and gives him a moment or two.

You alright son?

IQBAL: Yes. Thank you.

IQBAL leaves and OFFICER KELLY turns the lights out.

SNAP TO BLACK.